KISS THIS FLORIDA,

I'M OUTTA HERE

Diary of a Solo, Full-Time Rver

By: Joei Carlton Hossack

Skeena Press
P.O. Box 19071,
Sarasota, Florida
34276-2071

November 29, 2001.

To Joan.

We pass this way
only once. Enjoy
the journey

Joei Carlton Hossack

Published By: Skeena Press
                     P.O. Box 19071,
                     Sarasota, Florida 34276-2071

Copyright   June, 2000 Joei Carlton Hossack

Cover Design: Ralph Roberts
                     Alexander Books – a Division of Creativity,
                     Inc.

ISBN: 0-9657509-2-2

Library of Congress: 00-090236

Printed in USA
Printing: 10 9 8 7 6 5 4 3 2

Dedicated to Mary Mau.

Without her help, I'd still be packing the truck.

To my friends and family who worry about me and my chosen lifestyle.

IF ALL GOES WELL, I HAVE A GOOD TIME.

IF IT DOES NOT GO WELL, I HAVE A NEW BOOK.

Prologue

Just because I do what I want, when I want to and for as long as I like.

And just because I like what I'm doing, when I'm doing it and for the length of time that I'm doing it -----

DOESN'T MEAN I'M NOT WORKING.

Chapter 1

The Decision

Enough already, I said to myself. Your friends are sick to death of hearing how awful it is here. Do something about it or shut up.

I actually got stranded in Florida. I have, in recent years, compared myself to Alexandr Solzhenitsyn. When he got off the plane in Siberia, the most desolate region in the Soviet Union, he kissed the ground. Was exile in Vermont so terrible? Was being stranded in Sarasota, Florida every winter so terrible? For those sitting ass deep or worse in that white fluffy stuff that looks so pristine in pictures, Sarasota, on Florida's Gulf Coast, would be a dream come true. I however kissed the ground in whatever country I landed in every summer since Florida, for those not accustomed to the heat and humidity, was a notch below hell.

The stranding occurred a short time after my husband, Paul and I had purchased a large condo in April of 1992. It was to be our winter home. That was where we would store our "stuff" as George Carlin put it. We would satisfy our wanderlust by traveling the world in the summertime and golf, fish, volunteer our services and generally live a stationary life to the fullest of our ability in the wintertime. We gradually moved all our belongings into our new home in early May, lived in the home from the fourteenth to the sixteenth of that month and took off on another fantastic jaunt.

We stayed in Canada long enough for medical and dental appointments, to attend the wedding party of my nephew Stephen and his bride-to-be, Ruth, and to say goodbye to our friends and family. We returned to Great Britain. We retrieved our Renault Trafic motorhome that had been stored at the Barry docks just south of Cardiff, Wales. Sixteen days into what was to have been a four-and-a-half month trip, Paul

1

died of a heart attack in a campground in Northern Germany. Our winter home became my millstone.

For years I complained. "Florida would never have been the spot I would have chosen to be alone in," I moaned to my friends.

"So get out," they said.

"The people here are too old," I griped to anyone within earshot who would listen.

"So get out," they said.

"If Paul were alive," I bellyached, "we would have been out of here a long time ago."

"So get out," they said.

"I can't stand all this traffic anymore," I cried, wallowing in self-pity.

"So get out," they said.

As the years passed, I transformed myself into an author with numerous newspaper articles to my credit. I did feature writing for a Sarasota magazine called Writer's Guidelines and News and wrote two books in my spare time. Restless From The Start, a collection of short stories was released April 1997 and Everyone's Dream Everyone's Nightmare, the two and a half year adventure of roaming the world with my husband was released November 1998. Thanks to my needing a new career (or more importantly a new life) and forcing myself to join the speaking organization called Toastmasters International, I became comfortable entertaining throngs with my amusing accounts of traveling the world solo. I knew in my heart that the time had come. I had to get out.

Months before the final decision and ultimate action I had had a brainstorm of an idea. The exotic places in the world that I now wanted to visit would be better suited in the winter. I would rent out my furnished residence during the high season, collecting a small fortune in advance, and I would occupy the place during the off season, spending my time profitably by working.

"Everything is air conditioned," they said.

"You can get anywhere in ten minutes, there's no traffic," they said.

"We like it better in the summer than in the winter because the pace is so much slower and more relaxed," they said.

"Everything is on sale and much cheaper," they said.

I don't remember exactly who "they" are, but as soon as I figure it out, I will strangle them with my bare hands and then kiss them for nudging me (as if a person can be nudged with a two-by-four) toward my ultimate goal of getting out.

By the end of May, that ill-fated summer of 1997, the heat soared to what I discovered was a normal ninety-five degrees but that was okay. June, still around ninety-five degrees with a little rain thrown in for good measure, was still okay. It was no more than six or seven occasions that ten inches or more fell in one day nearly drowning us on the streets. July around ninety-five degrees was okay because the few friends I had left were away for a couple of months and I didn't leave my air conditioned abode much. August at ninety-five degrees, I must confess, was starting to get on my nerves. Somehow I was still managing. By September, at ninety-five degrees, it was no longer safe to be standing in front of my air conditioned car that had been parked in front of my air conditioned condo and used to go to the air conditioned movie theater, the air conditioned supermarket and the air conditioned restaurant since I had visions of running someone down just for the sport of it.

There were other problems that reared up on their eight, ten or a hundred legs and bit me that first and only summer of my discontent. Just for a bit of diversity, our Toastmasters' meeting was held at an outdoor gazebo on one of the ten most beautiful beaches in the world, Siesta Key, a stone's throw from Sarasota. My feet, covered by the barest of sandals, were immediately attacked by things too small to be seen without a magnifying glass and the sprays that everyone, except me, seemed to carry in their purse, pouch or pocket had no affect whatsoever. My fingernails tore at my flesh. Trying to concentrate on the meeting was a joke and I couldn't leave because I played a key role in the program. The split second the gavel hit the podium declaring the meeting adjourned, I sprinted through the parking lot howling like a banshee, fumbling for my car keys. I could not wait to get into a bathtub and scrub away at whatever tiny jaws had been biting. The next day I could not get my shoes on due to the swelling and the day after that I had what looked like a thousand tiny oozing infections. That was the start of things to come.

The incident was still fresh in my mind when I was bitten by either six fire ants or one voracious ant that bit me six times. I had been out on my driveway washing my car while wearing those same damn sandals. I went into an allergic reaction almost immediately. My skin suddenly became very hot and itchy. Angry red hives started breaking out all over my body starting at my armpits. Panicked, I jumped into my car and drove to the nearest drug store less than a mile away.

The pharmacist, after inspecting my neck, underarms and the back of my legs that were now swollen, hot and rock-hard, suggested Benedryl. Even before ringing up my purchase on the cash register he handed me a paper cup with water and a couple of the pills from the box he had just opened. The pills halted the allergic reaction immediately but left me leery of every creeping or crawling tiny creature.

Fortunately the fire ant is the only tiny creature in Florida. The rest of the native insect population leave footprints in the sand. They are large enough to produce nightmares only Spielberg could imagine despite their deceivingly cute names. Palmetto bug springs to mind.

Palmetto, a district just north of Sarasota I must assume gave the creature it's name or, heaven forbid, the other way around. If these gigantic, disease-spreading inhabitants had stayed put in their own district they would not have been a problem for me. The Palmetto bug however is so large it could walk or fly or jump anywhere it wanted to in just a few days. And unfortunately they do.

They have few worldly possessions which is why they want mine.....or yours. The family migration includes spouses, millions of children, friends and in-laws in the hopes of resettling someplace lush and preferably damp which is definitely not a problem in mid-western Florida. I'm sure, without paying for the privilege, they also hop onto buses and sneak into train compartments and occasionally travel as stars of the show with the circuses attracting attention, along with raves, everywhere they go. When a live one jumps out at you in your home, the pest control companies have you at their mercy. Without going into details, trust me on that last one.

Palmetto bugs reside only in Florida. The rest of the world calls them as they see them.....cockroaches. Somehow, even with hordes the bugs, I managed.

The day beyond redemption was September 12, 1997. I opened the door of my condo a little after lunch hoping for a half-hour walk to the post office. The heat and humidity hit me like a blast from an open coal furnace and my life, as I knew it, was over. I slammed the door and stood with clenched fists, feeling the flimsy door and its frame vibrate. The rage had been slowly building up over the months. "I'm a God damned prisoner in this place," I swore as I stomped back to the couch, my computer and work. I didn't leave the house until nightfall.

At the community swimming pool the next morning I sat beside a real estate agent also living at Strathmore. I suggested she bring over a contract some time at her convenience that day and the five and a half years of indecision and immobility was over.

A plan of action was set in motion. That afternoon, Colleen McGray from Bob Ray and Associates sat across from me at my dining room table. A contract was set before me along with a computer print out of all the other villas at Strathmore Riverside Villas (SRV for short) that were for sale or sold, along with size, asking and/or sold price.

A cursory glance at the standard contract along with more of an explanation than was necessary and the deed was done. I would be out before I could blink my eye or at least by the end of a short nap. "Things are selling fast," she said.

Listening to music in the cafe at Barnes & Noble on Tamiami Trail that evening, I was seated at a table with dear friends Sunny Greenberg and Charlie Schnee. Not wanting to interfere with the music, I wrote Sunny a note, "I put my condo up for sale today."

"Where are you going?" the written question was passed back to me.

"I don't know," I responded.

"You get two weeks with kitchen privileges," the note continued.

I patted her hand in appreciation. I had met Sunny in a bereavement group five years before each of us having recently lost our husbands. Sunny knew from the first time we met that I desperately wanted out of "God's waiting room" and only now had the courage to do something about it.

Later that night the conversation would be repeated almost word for word over the telephone with my friends Joan and Cary Dressler in Hudson, Quebec, with only one minor change. When I responded, "I don't know" to the "where are you going" question, Cary reminded me of the old Jewish proverb "God will provide."

Not being able to reach my sister because of her erratic work schedule and a three hour time difference, I wrote her a letter telling her of my plans to get out of Florida. Again I said that I had no idea where I would be going and told of Cary's remark about "God will provide" and added "just in case He didn't Sunny Greenberg will."

An enormous weight was taken off my shoulders with the signing on the dotted line. Being realistic I knew it would take some time to get the place sold because my agent would be on holidays in Germany for three weeks and while she was gone I would be returning to Canada for a month or more. Left clean and neat and cool, my place would be shown while I was away thanks to multiple listings and an agent who would be refreshed from her holidays. I could look forward to many bids when I returned, Colleen had guaranteed. I left addresses and telephone numbers in Canada just in case I had serious buyers that could not wait my return.

No such luck. I returned to Florida early November and discovered the place exactly as I had left it. There had not been an open house for agents nor for potential buyers. The house had been shown only twice and my agent had not set foot onto the property since my departure. I was devastated.

I told my tale of woe to anyone who would listen and amongst the listeners was my friend Helen Zubrine.

"Fire her," Helen said.

"I can't do that," I answered. "I signed a contract and it doesn't expire until the thirteenth of December."

"Read your contract," Helen insisted. "It must say that she will show your property. She didn't do that. Get rid of her."

Sleep did not come easily that night. I tossed and turned and at five in the morning I was sitting at my computer composing a letter to my real estate agent. At seven I was on the phone reading the letter to Helen who suggested a few minor changes and by nine, on my way out to a lecture that I was giving at the Holmes Beach Library, I delivered the letter to Colleen. A copy of the letter would be delivered to the manager of her company that afternoon on my way home from the lecture. I could do nothing else but go through my day as if it were a normal one.

That afternoon I delivered the letter to the office of Bob Ray and Associates on Siesta Key and Colleen was doing desk duties. She got both copies of the letter. She suggested we talk about it.

"What did I say in that letter that wasn't true?" I asked not really expecting an answer since the look on my face was murderous.

"The manager is letting you out of the contract," she said, her voice subdued and expressionless. "Go ahead and hire another agent."

"I want that in writing," I said, "please let me know when it's ready. I'll pick it up. I have already wasted too

7

much time with you and this company," I almost spat the words out at her.

Early the next morning, a telephone call from Colleen told me that the paperwork was ready and I could pick it up at her home, walking distance from my own. Within five minutes I had the necessary paperwork and within fifteen minutes I had the name of another agent also living in Strathmore. Jackie Davison had sold my neighbor's villa within a week. That was good enough for me. I called her office, spoke to her for less than a minute and hired her over the phone. She came by early the following morning. I told Jackie that between six in the morning and midnight the place was open to anyone who might be interested. That privilege was used and abused on several occasions but I didn't care. For every person who saw the place it became one step closer to freedom.

My condo became Grand Central Station from the minute I signed the new contract. By the following weekend there had been two open houses for agents and a third one for buyers. Strangers were traipsing through at all hours of the day and night but still there were no acceptable bids. I refused two bids where I was expected to hold the mortgage. Since I counted on selling the place during the high season and time seemed to be marching on, it didn't take long for me to become discouraged. My friend Joe Burke provided me with the answer.

"Pray," he said. "My prayers have always been answered. I haven't always needed what I prayed for," he assured me, "but they've all been answered. I have learned to pray for what I need," he confessed. "Trust me," he said. "It works."

What did I have to lose? Ranting, raving and cursing hadn't helped much. I started praying daily for what I needed and ended each prayer with "please send me a buyer for my condo," just in case He didn't think I really needed it.

I returned from a Toastmasters' meeting one Wednesday night and found five messages on my machine from my agent with instructions to call at any hour the minute I walked in.

At ten o'clock, the night of the seventh of January 1998 I called Joe. "I just got a bid on my house. The agent is coming over and I'm told it's an acceptable bid. Joe," I said, "I think she's a nun."

"Now I'm really impressed," Joe returned my banter. "You ask for God's help and He sends you one of His own."

Before midnight, with the agent going back and forth over the phone with the potential buyer and her agent, we had an agreement. Although the buyer had asked for a first of April closing, she agreed immediately to a February seventeenth closing with the condition that I lease the property back until the thirty-first of March.

The agreement was perfect.

Chapter 2

The First Honest Tradesman

It didn't take long for me to go into a panic mode. I had five weeks to kill until I was sure that I would be getting out the place. It would be five weeks of slow and painful torture. I worried about everything and I worried constantly. Since I could never bring myself to upgrade any part of the condo, except for painting the lanai a dark green and a bit of ceramic tiling in the kitchen and hallway, I looked at everything as a potential disaster waiting to happen.

I was sure that the inspection, paid for by the buyer, would reveal an expensive hazard lurking inside every cupboard, behind every wall and under each floorboard, except of course there were no floorboards. Like most of the Florida homes, under my old, drab carpeting was a poured concrete slab. The angels must have been with me when the inspection was done. Three minor problems, that I was (mostly) able to correct myself, were listed.

The first infraction that needed corrective surgery was taking the protective film, that kept the sun from heating the inside of my home to a thousand degrees, off the windows. Most windows that faced the morning sun had bubbled and cracked years before. Our SRV book of rules affectionately referred to as "The Bible" indicated that I was in major violation. I had been in violation since the day the first tiny bubble appeared on the window and that was probably the very same instant that I signed on the bottom line purchasing the condo. I was now however compelled to remove it.

I called several window companies. Most quoted a price of twenty-five dollars per window at the minimum. At the thought of having to spend close to a thousand dollars I panicked. Like a mad woman I went racing into Home Depot. They were famous for providing brochures, free classes and information on almost everything. Surely they would have something available on the subject. I latched onto the first available salesman and spewed out my tale of woe

I was now armed with step by step directions. They were supplied by the young fellow, whose sleeve I held onto for dear life, just in case he decided to flee the scene. I purchased a window scraping handle costing one dollar ninety-five cents plus an extra box of two-sided, flat, square razor blades for seventy-five cents. I returned home. I was prepared to spend the next five weeks taking care of this most expensive problem.

It was definitely not the most fun I had ever had however it turned out to be a much needed, stress relieving project. With over thirty louvered windows involved, two large picture windows and four small rectangular ones, every free daylight minute was spent stripping one or two of them. Much of the darkened film came off in one swoop taking the gummy portion with it. The rest came off in bits and pieces sometimes needing a bit of extra muscle to remove the sticky backing. The task was so mindless, needing only hand and arm movement it turned out to be rather relaxing.

I dragged my portable black-and-white television set from room to room allowing it to drone on in the background. I stopped to watch for a few minutes any time my arm needed a rest or when something on the "eye" caught my attention. In the end it turned out to be a real accomplishment and cost only pennies.

The second problem turned out to be a little more expensive then the first. I required a plumber to disconnect an old water softener that had been out of commission long before we bought the property. The plumber took care of rerouting the outside copper tubing then snipped some little wire that connected the softener to the fuse box.

"You'll need an electrician to remove the live wire that I just cut," he warned. "I could do it," he said. "But I'm not allowed."

"That's okay, I'll pay you extra to do it," I volunteered.

"It's really easy. It'll just takes a minute, but I can't," he said. "I'm not insured for it" he insisted, "but it's really easy."

"Oh come on," I cajoled, "just do it."

"It's really easy, but I'm sorry, I can't," he repeated. "It'll just take a minute," he said. "I can give you the name of an electrician," he volunteered.

This guy was really starting to piss me off.

It was early the next morning when I dragged out the yellow pages and started calling electricians listed alphabetically and starting with the number that had the same first three digits as my number. The charge would be anywhere from thirty to sixty dollars an hour but no one I spoke to was available anytime soon. Frustrated and getting nowhere with the phone book, I was looking up the number of a friend, living at our complex, hoping to ask for advice. One little ad "seeking electrical work" in our SRV directory caught my attention. I left a message on his answering machine. He called back that evening. His price was thirty dollars per hour and he would be working in our complex the next day but was really busy.

I explained the problem and he too assured me that it would not take long.

"I'm up really early. Why don't you stop by here before you start your day, six, seven in the morning would be all right. I don't mind," I answered, "I'll be up."

"Okay," he said, "let me see what I can do."

There was a knock at the door a little before eight the next morning. He was a young fellow, early thirties, with an easy, genuine smile. I lead him around to the back yard and watched as experienced fingers opened the gray fuse box door that hung on the wall behind the condo. With a tiny screwdriver, only slightly larger than the one I would use to tighten the screw on my glasses, he loosened the screw. With thumb and forefinger he plucked out the offending live wire. He tightened the screw. He closed the fuse box.

I was sick. This is what I had spent a day on the phone trying to arrange. This is what was going to cost me thirty dollars plus traveling expenses. This one-minute job from the front door of my condo to completion that the plumber could have handled but was not insured for was going to cost me thirty bucks.

"Come on in," I said, suddenly feeling nauseated.

"That's okay," he said, "I can't charge you for this."

"Sorry but I need you to sign the form left by the plumber that says it was done by a professional," I said. I was now sure he would refuse without some payment since he was putting his John Hancock on an official document.

"Sure," he said without hesitation, giving me a shy, almost embarrassed smile. I led the way into my living room via the back door and through my screened and glassed lanai.

After he signed, I handed him a ten-dollar bill and thanked him for his service. He held up his hand to refuse but I thanked him again and suggested he have a beer on me when his day was done. Six long and frustrating years in Florida and I had just found my first honest tradesman. His timing was perfect.

Set before me now was another of those mindless tasks. This one however was somewhat backbreaking. The plumber would have charged me fifty dollars an hour for digging out the recently disarmed water softener. I decided, after he had set my blood pressure to the point of a slow rolling boil with his "it'll only take a minute routine," that the exercise would be me more good than harm. I would try to do the job myself.

Armed with a variety of sizes and shapes of borrowed shovels, I started digging out the one foot square, beige, hard plastic box that had been set deep into the ground. With about six inches on one side now within easy reach I tried smashing pieces of it with a hammer. I only succeeded in hurting myself when my body acted as a shock absorber and didn't even put a dent in the plastic. I continued digging the hard packed earth for about a half-hour, uncovering part way down one side. I took a break for a couple of days since manual labor was tough on my untrained body at any time and besides, I thought, it wasn't going anywhere. I returned one cool late afternoon to dig out a second side. Since much of the casing was filled with rainwater I had no idea how far down I would be digging. After one half-hour session on my third or fourth day it suddenly gave way. Instant euphoria. A little more digging around all three sides and I pulled the box out intact. Tipping it away from the house, I poured out the foul, mosquito infested water and dragged the two foot deep, half inch thick, plastic box, complete with broken bits and pieces to the front of my condo to wait for the garbage truck to pick up. I returned to the back of the house to shovel some of the loose dirt into the gaping hole. After a shower and some clean clothes I returned to Home Depot to purchase a couple of bags of earth to fill the chasm.

One last job lay ahead. Two of the window opening crank handles had broken and would no longer open and close the louvered windows on the lanai. With my recent experience as a Jill-of-all-trades I was sure I could do the job myself. I carefully removed the three screws that held the handle along with the metal housing into the window frame. I went outside to remove the metal arm that connected it to the device that made all four windows open or close at the same time. I made sure both cranks were the same and returned to Home Depot for what seemed like the thousandth time. I was stunned. There must have been fifty varieties. There were left handed and right handed openers. There were openers with two screws and some with three screws. There were some with three holes that didn't match the holes that I had on mine. There were openers with a short, fat arm. There were openers with a long, thin arm. There were metal ones and plastic ones and there were combinations of the two.

"Who the hell designed this window opener," I said to a couple standing close enough to hear my mutterings. They had been watching me sitting on the floor with the load of hardware scattered all around me, comparing pieces. I concluded it was certainly no one with a brain that was in use for any length of time.

Going through each of the possibilities took over an hour. I purchased a couple only after I was guaranteed that if they didn't fit I could return them. The new handles fit and took only a few minutes to install. Unfortunately I needed different bolts for the outside since the ones that came with the setup didn't fit. I had to dig some out of an old jar of bits and pieces that my husband kept.

When all three jobs were taken care of in record time, I went back to worrying. I was so sure that things were going too smoothly and something would fall apart, leak, break, cave-in or worse yet, that the buyer would back out at the last minute. Something.

Chapter 3

A Wise Choice - I Hope

While I worried, I window-shopped and dreamed. My friend Mary Mau and I drifted through the RV show held in Tampa, Florida in early January. We ferreted out and wandered into and out of every motorhome that I felt I would be able to afford after the sale of my condo. Even though I owned it outright, there wasn't going to be a lot of money to spend on something as luxurious as a real home on wheels. We admired motorhomes costing more money than I had in this world and, of course with one of the biggies, I would have needed time to find a tall, broad-shouldered blond stud to hire as my own private toy boy that would drive it for me. We looked at campers that I felt I could live in on a full time basis, complete with a full-time ready-made bed, something that was not always available in many of the smaller rigs. We looked at motorhomes with slide outs, the latest craze. We looked at ones with baby-soft genuine leather seats and an apartment-sized washer and dryer. There were vehicles with full-length mirrors screwed onto every cabinet door and tract lighting on the walls and ceiling and befitting a brothel making house calls. We looked. We talked. We planned. We laughed at the ones costing a million or more.

"Anything needing that many cleansers," Mary said pointing to one of the super expensive ones with the side panel open, displaying fifteen or twenty spray bottles, cans and scouring pads for the many different cleaning jobs, "you don't want."

"You're right," I said. "Besides it doesn't matter how much it costs someone still has to go outside, rain or shine, and connect or clean the damn sewer hose," I reminded her. We had a hearty, nervous laugh over that one.

The motorhomes costing all of the proceeds from the sale of the condo were approximately twenty to twenty-four feet long and I knew I could managed that size easily. Mary and I each took a brochure along with prices and dealers' addresses of all the ones that looked interesting. Every dealer had the best motorhome. Every dealer was willing to bargain. Every dealer had show specials. Every dealer would drop another thousand or two if I bought that day. Mary and I left more confused than we had arrived. We drove the scenic way home taking some of the back roads that I had never seen before.

We spent several days digging through the pile of brochures, discarding many. We visited dealers in Nokomis, Bradenton and Venice to see what they had in stock. The more we looked and the more we were pressured by the salesmen, the more aggravating it became. None of the motorhomes we looked at would accommodate the thousand or more books that I would be dragging along with me.

What also became apparent was that I would have to unhook the water, sewer, electricity and cable for each trip. Just a short hop to the grocery store for a carton of milk would require more work than I wanted to think about. The bottom line fell in like a ton of bricks. I would have to pull my car, an emerald green 1993 Ford Escort Wagon.

"Well," I told Mary one day while we were soaking in her outdoor hot tub, "if I have to pull something, I want it to be new. I don't really want to but I might as well have a look at a few fifth wheel trailers."

A couple of weeks later we went to another Recreational Vehicle (RV) show in Tampa. This was a much bigger show than the last with many more companies showing their wares, more specials and the same aggressive salesmen. We trudged up and down every row. We talked to every salesman from every dealership who was featuring small fifth wheels. Under no circumstances could I be talked into even looking at the twenty-six footers or larger. It sent chills up my spine thinking about handling any fifth wheel, let alone something that seemed monstrous in size. Whatever I was looking at didn't even take into consideration the length of the truck. I looked at them all and tried to keep from panicking. It wasn't easy.

After listening to a half-hour presentation by Joe and Vicki Kieva, the RVing Guru couple, talking about the life of a full-time RVer, we were ready to call it quits for the day.

"We haven't been up that aisle," Mary said pointing up some side street crammed with more of the same.

"We've been up and down every aisle," I assured her, sounding a little discouraged since they had all started looking alike hours before and I really hadn't seen anything that I really wanted.

"No," she repeated, "I'm sure of it. We haven't seen this last row."

On the last street, in the last hour, on legs that felt like rubber from all our slow walking and climbing of either two or three steps, I found exactly what I was looking for.....a twenty-two and a half foot, fifth wheel Wanderer by Thor. It was one of the new lightweight models that had all, or what I thought was all, the amenities. The interior had an attractive dark green/mauve color scheme with the open concept that we had only seen on larger models. It came with a two-year bumper-to-bumper guarantee including appliances. It was in my price range.

The salesman promised lessons, several days of free camping in their own campground in St. Augustine, Florida and I would not be allowed on the road until I was comfortable pulling. NOTE: Please remember that last promise as I progress into the book.

I was told that a fully refundable down payment would guarantee the show price. I told him I would take my chances. I'll make all decisions after the sale goes through on the condo, I told him. He was not pleased with that last development. I must have looked like a chicken ready to be plucked.

Again we took the long way home. We talked excitedly all the way. We stopped for dinner at a little roadside café. We stopped for ice cream. It had turned out to be an uplifting and fruitful day.

All I needed now was for the sale to go through.

Within a day or two of my fifth wheel decision, Mary and I were out looking at trucks. I wanted big. I wanted powerful. I wanted diesel. Memories of my Volkswagen Westphalia flooded my mind when I remembered climbing some mountain in Wyoming with a motorhome that coughed and spluttered up every mole hill. To add to my terror in that Wyoming incident was that it coughed and spluttered on the way down the other side. I felt sure I would be stranded alone somewhere up in snow country. I never wanted to ever feel that powerless (if you'll excuse the pun) again.

Mary and I returned to several of the car dealerships. We drove to Tampa. We drove to Bradenton. We drove to Venice. We drove to Port Charlotte. We looked at Dodge. We looked at Chevrolet. We looked at Ford. We were killing the time effectively and with each passing day I became more and more agitated and uptight.

Long before the closing, I settled on the Ford F-250 Powerstroke Diesel for a number of reasons, the least of them being that there were a million of them out on the road. A second consideration was that the Ford was ten thousand dollars cheaper than the Dodge.

The weeks of waiting were unsettling but it was all I could do. I waited.

Chapter 4

Freedom

In those last days of condo living I was mildly confused, borderline, and I use that term loosely, manic-depressive and totally frustrated. I didn't want to start selling off my possessions just in case it would jinx the closing.....or worse. I knew if that happened I would spend the rest of my life in an empty condo that no one wanted because they could not visualize the fifteen hundred and ten square feet with furniture. I didn't want to sit there surrounded by everything I owned in this world and then have to get rid of it all in one swoop. Needless to say I drove myself crazy.

Sometime during that last gut wrenching, nail biting week a special friend called one afternoon to thank me for the travel lecture I had given to the women's group where she was a member. I spoke candidly to her about my fears that the condo would not sell.

"Why do you say it won't sell?" Anita Simons asked, so sure that I would give her a long list of reasons and problems.

"Because the deal is so perfect it scares me," I answered. "No problems.....nothing, just a sweet perfect deal."

"Stop worrying," she said without a moment's hesitation. "The universe is a perfect place," she said, "and if everything is going smoothly then it is meant to be." This she guaranteed.

For some reason or other her words or probably her attitude seemed to ease my troubled mind. With less than a week left to wait I needed to cling to any words of wisdom.

It was six days after my birthday and one day after the Presidents' birthdays. It was a Tuesday on that glorious day of February 17, 1998. The birds were singing the sweetest song. The flowers were in full bloom. The sun was shining. Even if it wasn't I would have seen only sunshine. I was tiptoeing on cloud nine knowing that it was all coming to an end that day and I had survived.....bruised, battered and beaten.....but alive to tell the tale.

Tuesday was also the day I would normally meet my writing group at two in the afternoon but this day was special. If we were going to meet at all it would have to be earlier in the day. Since my friends did not want me to be chewing my nails all alone, our writing group consisting of Sally Fradkin, Al Cooke, the person I blame for every editing mistake in my book, Joe Burke, and myself met around lunch time.

We ate at El Adobe on Tamiami Trail, a group favorite for Mexican cuisine. Since my stomach was already churning from the tension, I treated myself to a salad with jumbo shrimp. Afterwards we headed across the street to Barnes & Noble to continue our meeting in the confines of their coffee shop. They listened to me rant and rave for awhile longer then Sally, a science fiction writer, read one of her short stories. I tried to concentrate on her contribution, without much success, before Al read one of his. We critiqued and discussed both as another hour slipped by. At every opportunity I checked my watch, tapping it from time to time, to make sure it was still working. Long before the appointed hour, I left.

I arrived at the lawyer's office well ahead of the group and waited nervously in the outer office. Fortunately a number of magazines that I hadn't seen before were available. The one on luxury travel held my attention the longest since there wasn't much reading and lots of colorful pictures to hold my waning attention span. My eyes darted around with every movement or sound.

I had been told that the buyer had been through my condo on a number of occasions so I was certain that I would recognize her. My agent arrived surrounded by a group of people that did not look even vaguely familiar. The lawyer, the buyer and her agent were all strangers to me. As soon as we were seated, a mound of paperwork was presented by the secretary. The lawyer opened the folder.

That was not a sonic boom you heard at precisely three-thirty in the afternoon on that day. That was the instant I was handed the check for the complete selling price of the condo. Complete less real estate fees, taxes, stamps, the insurance policy I had purchased on the appliances and six weeks worth of rent since I had agreed to lease the property back from the new owner. The complete price was enough to buy a large load of groceries, a fabulous dinner or an economy flight out of Florida.

The noise was the weight of the world slipping off my shoulders and crashing to the floor. At that moment I didn't care if the roof of the condo collapsed. It wasn't mine. I take that back.....temporarily I still needed a roof over my furniture.

I was free.

When all the paperwork was signed we said goodbye at the bottom of the stairs. The new owner, my landlady temporarily, asked if she could bring workmen by to inspect, to measure and to prepare quotes.

"Sure, anytime," I answered. "Just give me a call." I walked back to my car a foot above the ground. There was a certain lightness in my step that I had not known in years.

"I'm free," my heart sang in that brief moment of euphoria.

On the way to Mary's house, I stopped at the bank and purchased a one-week Certificate of Deposit for the entire amount. Mary was waiting for me. She handed me a glass of white wine when I walked through the front door. I flopped onto her overstuffed couch in the living room.

"It's over. I'm free," was all I could say.

There were no tears. There was no joy. There was only relief.

Chapter 5

Headaches, Backaches and Pains in the Ass

The wine was not enough to settle me down. I definitely needed some kind of mini celebration even though my nerves were frayed and I was very uptight. "Do you want to go out to dinner?" I asked.

Always game for a meal out and knowing my fragile state of mind, she answered "sure" without giving it a second thought.

"Let's meet at the Sarasota Brewing Company in a couple of hours for a burger or whatever," I volunteered.

The pub was another of our favorite eating spots. We were always assured good food, fast and efficient service, friendly people around and since I had deposited the entire check from the closing of the condo, it was relatively inexpensive. I had actually asked the bank manager if I could deposit the entire check less one dollar five cents for bus fare but she had laughed at that suggestion. The laughter had eased a little of my tension.

I drove home. I opened the door and unceremoniously stepped inside. Everything was exactly as I had left it that morning but somehow it felt different. It felt distant like I had entered the exact home but on another planet. It all looked drab and colorless. It felt empty or perhaps I was the one that was empty.

I took a bath. I changed my clothes and made a few phone calls letting a few friends know that the dirty deed was done. I left for the Brewing Company. Even though I was much earlier than I should have been Mary was waiting for me.

The days, the weeks, and the months had been an emotional roller coaster for me. A headache lurked behind each good time and each glass of wine so even with this celebration I passed on a second glass of wine. We celebrated quietly and talked a lot, one minute very excited, the next subdued and reflective.

As desperately as I wanted out, I had no idea what I had let myself in for. All I knew was that I was getting out. Of that I was now blissfully and absolutely certain. The weeks ahead were loaded with headaches, backaches and major pains in the ass. Since my life was suddenly plunged into total chaos and for the sake of the book, some sense must be made of it, let us start with:

HEADACHES:

Two days before the closing of the condo I learned that my dear friend Buddy had died in Canada earlier in February and I was being asked to say a few words at the memorial service being held at his winter home on Siesta Key. Before I got off the phone with his companion of twenty-five years I had the start of my first "classic" migraine with wiggly lines and flashing lights to terrify me.

The day after the closing I test drove the Ford F-250 diesel for the first time. It was big, noisy and not easily handled. Before I had gone five miles down a side street I had my second "classic" migraine headache. This time wiggly lines, flashing lights and the new dimension of giant black holes, obliterating a person's leg and one entire limb of a tree, added to the terror. On both occasions everything vanished within a half-hour leaving me to wonder if I was losing my mind. Neither incident came with the severe pain normally associated with my migraine headache.

The Florida based distributor for my first book Restless From The Start had never paid me. After months of writing, waiting, calling and talking politely to them I was now having screaming fits on the phone with them on a daily basis. Two days before leaving Florida I received a check for half the amount owed. It arrived in an envelope that had been torn open and partially resealed with transparent tape, scribbled on and with the wrong address. The check was intact. I cashed it immediately. To my amazement it didn't bounce.

24

After checking out most of the Ford dealerships between Tampa and Venice I contacted a local dealer in Nokomis since the manager of the truck division was a friend of a friend. He vowed to give me the best deal. After ordering the vehicle complete with a heavy duty towing package, CD player and dual air bags (that last item written in bold pen across my receipt), and leaving a hundred dollar deposit, I returned home to work on getting full-time RVing insurance. It was through the insurance company that I learned that the vehicle I had just purchased did not have dual air bags. It did not even have a driver side air bag. The only air bag, it seems, had been the manager.

"I guess I owe you one," said Mr. Lowlife when I called and confronted him.

Also concerning the purchase of the truck was the fact that I had been charged two hundred dollars for a new license plate. I had been advised that the plates on my Ford Escort wagon were not transferable. At the Department of Motor Vehicles, after they canceled the plates on my car, I learned they were indeed transferable.

Putting into print exactly what I had told the manager would remove this book from the travel section and banish it to the adult section of some seedy bookstore just off the main drag. Let us just say that within three days I received a one hundred and forty-six dollar check in the mail along with a letter that started with "In reviewing your file......"

I drove back to my (now) rental unit with my brand new possession on the twenty-seventh of February, the day my husband would have been fifty-eight years old. Within a few hours an SRV warning ticket was placed on the windshield reminding me that trucks were not allowed at the villas. For a two-week period only the truck could be parked in the main lot near the clubhouse, located within easy reach about half a mile from where I lived. In the end it was resolved but not before letters, telephone calls and threats had been exchanged with management, office staff, members of the board, and anyone else within earshot. This last item will be listed again under the PAIN IN THE ASS section.

BACKACHES:

Before I start bellyaching, there are friends to whom I will be forever indebted. Mary Mau, my auburn hair, green-eyed, Irish delight, who when I asked how she would like to be described in my book responded "LUSH." (Note: In my New Comprehensive Crossword Dictionary lush is described as juicy, succulent, luxuriant. In my New Webster Pocket Dictionary lush is described as having or covered with abundant growth. I am putting my friend Mary in that first category.) Your wish is my command. My lush friend, Mary, would have to be first. She will always be on my list of angels. I don't know what I would have done without her. Margaret and Doug Drew, whose company and friendship and help I thoroughly enjoyed and appreciated in both Sarasota and Toronto, Canada are right up there in the thank you category as well. Joe and Diane Burke, who started as writing friends and were soon elevated to friends always in my heart are also on that very short list of people I could not do without. These are the people that showed up to help sell, to price, to watch, or just to support at almost every sale day.

Not wanting to get rid of my stuff too early I waited a couple of weeks and then went into my panic mode. I advertised a three-day sale in several local newspapers and had flyers made up that I distributed door-to-door at SRV. I delivered the flyers to each of the three hundred and thirty-six ground floor villas in one outing. I knew that the minute I walked into my condo the phone would be ringing and I would be advised by someone on The Board of Directors, affectionately called The Condo Police or simply The Gestapo, that delivering door-to-door was not permitted at SRV. The task took over four hours. The phone was ringing when I walked through the door. I let the answering machine pick it up. This too will be listed again under the PAIN IN THE ASS section.

In those first sale days someone bought my bed, brass headboard and all. Most of the expensive pieces that Paul and I had collected over the years went in those early hours. Several who could not make up their mind returned later in the day hoping to bid on a few special pieces. They were disappointed when they were too late. The stuff they wanted was gone. By the end of the third day I could not believe how much had been sold. By the end of the third day I could not believe how much was left.

This was a horror and I was exhausted. I was too tired to even think about all the treasures I had given away for a pittance.

Lamps, pictures, a radio, bags of wool and craft supplies that had been left in the back bedroom, I brought into the living room and spread them around. Only a four piece, light-colored, all-wood bedroom set remained behind to fill the space. Recouped by mid week, I advertised another three-day sale and again delivered flyers around the complex. What the hell were they going to do to me, throw me out!

Again much of the stuff went and with each piece going out the door, I started feeling exhilarated.....and depressed.

Mary showed up every sale day sometimes with donuts and coffee, sometimes just to keep me company. We talked during the lulls.

By the end of the sixth day of selling, I had people telling me to call at the end and they would give me one price for the balance. I called. They had lied. They would come and cart it away. Surely I didn't expect any money for the balance. I turned them away. There was still too much to keep, too much to throw away and if I wanted to donate the lot, it certainly would not be to them. It would go to a worthy cause.

I took one more chance. I advertised a "No Reasonable Offer Refused" sale and again spent four hours wandering the entire area delivering flyers.

I must have been nuts. A few people showed up, fewer bought.

On my last day in the condo, I waited for Goodwill, their nine o'clock appointment long past. My phone had been

27

disconnected before I was awake.   Mary arrived in time to sit and stare at the bare walls with me. My next door neighbor invited me for lunch since Goodwill was over three hours late. I had already cleaned out the pantry and disconnected the refrigerator. There was no food in the house. Mary was invited to join us but she had eaten just before leaving home.
PAIN IN THE ASS:
All of it.

Chapter 6

I Was Getting Out

I was getting out.

With almost everything gone and just a few days left I really had to buckle down and get to work even though my energy level had sunk to an all time low. Depression closed in on me in every empty room. Each time I looked around I was reminded that this was not the way it was supposed to be. The condo was just going to be a place to keep our stuff as my husband and I wandered the world collecting stories, memories and treasures.

I forced myself to keep focused and moving. What meager possessions remained had to be sorted, cleaned, packed away or discarded. Everything I owned in this world was going with me. I was leaving nothing in Florida. I wanted no reason to return.

The few things left were stacked in little piles on my old mustard-yellow shag carpeting that should have been replaced years before. It didn't take long to spread out my mementos and start looking through my photograph albums that would be going into storage. Paul, flexing his muscles on a beach in Nassau, clad only in a skimpy brown and beige bathing suit. Paul, with his shirt slung over his shoulder, sitting on a deck chair in front of the two-story farmhouse that we owned, in Quebec. The weather was sunny and warm on that day in January so many years before but there was snow on the ground. Paul, on a fishing boat, with the guys from work and a big one on the line. His friends had pulled his pants down exposing his derriere and taking the picture that I now cradled in my hand, tears stinging my eyes. Paul, sitting on his favorite, bright orange towel on the black-sand beach, in the Canary Islands. I reached out my index finger to stoke his chin as I had done so often in life. I could almost feel him stick his chin out so I would know he was enjoying it and not stop. I sorted through my treasured pictures, peeling back the plastic to remove some of the best ones to take with me. I hurriedly packed the rest into a separate box before the day melted away with nothing being accomplished. I went back to work.

At the end of the day I packed one small canvas bag with a few necessities and threw it onto the front seat of my truck. I locked the front door of the condo and left. I moved to Mary's house on Siesta Key. She opened the garage door when she heard my truck pull onto her driveway. I drove as far in as it would go and discovered that she could not close the garage door. My truck, with its mini back seat and long bed box, was too long to fit. I would have to get everything into boxes and move them to the front door of my condo because all the loading would have to be done the morning I left. I could almost feel my body buckle under the weight of the task I had before me.

After another day of packing and sorting it was a pleasure to leave the emptiness and the loneliness that threatened to swallow me and return to the comfort of my dear friend's home. We spent an hour in the hot tub talking and planning and trying to ignore the fact that I was terrified at the thought of pulling a trailer for the first time.

That night we went out to a Greek restaurant on Sarasota's main street, Tamiami Trail. The souvlaki was good but I couldn't eat much. We talked about my upcoming adventurous life with a middle-aged, married couple sitting at the next table. I sounded so brave. If the terror showed through they never mentioned it.

The evening ended early with my falling asleep on the couch in the living room in front of the television set. Mary woke me in time for a good night's sleep in an unbelievably comfortable queen sized bed with private bath. Without the droning of the television set in the background, however, sleep eluded me.

Before returning to my condo early the next morning, I raided the Manhattan Bagel dumpster on The Trail for as many clean, small boxes that were available. I needed them for all the bits and pieces that were headed for the new fifth wheel trailer that I had ordered two weeks before. I packed everything and stacked whatever I could close to the front door trying to leave narrow aisles to get from room to room. What an endless, depressing, backbreaking chore and it all had to be completed before three that afternoon. A little exhilaration set in when I saw a light at the end of the tunnel. My relief was short lived.

I locked the door behind me for the last time. I drove back to Siesta Key. I showered, changed my clothes and Mary and I headed out the door, driving her car to El Adobe. This was the location of my going away party. My friends in the bar, including Mary's sister, Annie Duffy and the restaurant owner were eager for that party spirit that I was so famous for, my favorite line being "let the games begin" whenever I entered.

Nothing could lift my spirits that last day. One by one the group arrived.....Joan Papa, Bal Usefoff, Tom Landers, Jackie French, Joe and Diane Burke, all bearing mementos, along with a rather inappropriately dressed male blow-up doll to ride in the passenger seat of my truck. The gifts were for me to remember my Sarasota home and Mote Marine where I had volunteered for several years. Annie had prepared special finger foods that covered three tables. Good luck balloons were tied onto several chairs. Everyone made an effort but mostly we sat and stared at each other. Few words were spoken. There was nothing left to say.

I was getting out.

Chapter 7

The Day From Hell

It was a day from hell and I had been through more than my share of them in recent months. I had slept poorly, despite exhaustion, and before the sun was up I was wandering around the kitchen. I needed some coffee. The night before I had insisted that I could pack the truck alone so I didn't want to wake Mary.

My friend had not slept any better than I had. The slightest unfamiliar movement in her house and she was up. It was around six and still outside dark when we dressed. Still insisting that I could do the whole job myself, she finally said, "Okay, I'll just pick up some coffee and donuts for us and meet you over there."

By the time she arrived with our makeshift breakfast I had backed the truck into the carport and right up to the front door. I had lined the bottom of my truck with a huge, sea blue tarp. I had loaded the first bunch of boxes, jumped into the truck bed, placed the boxes at the far end and returned to the condo for a repeat performance. Before the second load was in place I knew that the job would be impossible without help. In the early morning dew my T-shirt and jeans were already clinging to me uncomfortably and I could feel myself welling up with tears. As desperate as I was to get out I had chosen a monumental task for myself.

"Let's sit for a few minutes and have our coffee. I bought us some chocolate covered donuts," Mary said, knowing I would not be able to resist.

"What would I ever do without you," I said, my bottom lip quivering.

"It's okay," she replied, her hands massaging my slumped shoulders.

Mary stayed and worked. It took three hours. She dragged from the house hoisting each piece, box or large black garbage bag up onto the truck bed and I, constantly hunched over, put them where I thought they would fit, cramming bits and pieces into every available open space. In the end two big items didn't fit. Like it or not, I would have to come back to Florida sometime. Mary took home a carved mahogany elephant coffee table from Ghana, Africa slated to go into storage and the golf clubs that I hoped to use when I had time to relax a bit. With both of us pushing and/or pulling we managed to get the table into the back seat of her car. The golf clubs fit snugly into her trunk.

The goodbye scene was an emotional but somber one. It was ten o'clock in the morning when I threw a gray tarp over everything and tied the lot down with bungy cords of every length, size and color available. Camera in hand Mary took some pictures that to this day she hasn't shown me. She said the deep depression and anguish showed alarmingly on my face. We hugged. We cried. I was still crying when I drove my overloaded truck onto Swift Road heading towards Interstate 75.

I was still on Swift Road when I realized that every gust of wind ballooned the tarp that covered my possessions, making seeing out the back window or the passenger side for cars sneaking up beside me, almost impossible. I pulled into a garage, filled up with diesel, and corrected the problem as best I could.

My mind was in turmoil as I drove. I stayed in the slow lane on the I-75 heading north. There wasn't much traffic and, for that, I was grateful. I was exhausted from the weeks of physical labor and lack of sleep. My depression eased a bit every time I realized that I was really out of that dreadful condo and that my life would soon be filled with new people and places. After every pleasant thought, a bit of the terror crept back in, since my self-imposed lifestyle change was now just hours away. I was still very apprehensive at the thought of pulling the trailer that I had already committed to, alone.

The four-hour drive to St. Augustine was relatively uneventful even with the nerve wracking hours of driving on the pot-holed highway that crossed the state diagonally.

Construction slowed the cars to a snail's pace and drivers, already annoyed at the delays, became aggressive the instant there was a clearing. These hotshots would weave in and out between the cars at every opportunity. By the time St. Augustine was within easy range I was again starting to relax, not realizing that my long, awful day had barely begun.

The salesman had supplied explicit directions and I found the dealership lot with no problems. An hour went by before my new trailer was paid for and all the necessary paperwork was done. A computer glitch prevented my post office box from being accepted as an address and the salesman went round and round the program trying to make it work. He eventually pressed the right key and the job was done.

I followed a blond kid in his black, polished Chevy truck to the campground and a couple of employees took less than ten minutes to explained how everything worked. Most of the information went in one ear and out the other never stopping to say hello to a brain that had been overloaded months before with worry and anxiety.

It was suggested that I work as quickly as possible to get the truck unloaded since they had to put the fifth wheel housing into the bed of the truck that afternoon. I was stunned. It had taken us three hours to load the truck. Another four hours was devoted to the drive cross-country. An hour had been spent with the dealer writing checks and doing paperwork. Eight seconds worth of time had been provided finding out how everything worked. And now I had to unload the truck as quickly as I could because they needed to take the truck away. I glared at them, not saying a word, until they walked away.

My shoulders slumped with the weight of the world on them. I started unloading, taking one of the smaller boxes into the trailer and placing it as far back on the upper bunk bed as I could. I worked at a pace that only someone working under extreme duress could understand. An hour later when you could not see beyond the mountain still in the bed of the truck they sent a couple of goons over from the office to help. The deed was done by five thirty in the afternoon.

I walked into my new home and discovered that if I wanted to sleep in my bed and, heaven forbid, if I had to use the bathroom during the night, I had better start unpacking and putting things away. My bed, the two bunk beds at the rear, the table, both bench seats were loaded with boxes, blocking the entrance into most of the cupboards, closets and bathroom. I sat down on the one vacant spot on the floor. My legs were tightly crossed and pressed up against several boxes and crates. I cried, deep, gasping sobs. This was an entire world with just me in it. I could do nothing else. I let the tears flow.

Slowly I forced myself upright, washed and dried my face and resolved to do only what I had to. I started checking out the boxes. The ones slated for storage had been marked "Storage" with a big black marker and I put those to one side. The others I opened one at a time and started putting things in the cupboards and closets and under the seats, discarding the empties right outside the door. I cleared the boxes away one by one until I could sleep in my bed and not trip on anything on the way to the bathroom.

It was after eight at night and dark. My truck had been returned hours before. I walked to the plaza just a couple of hundred yards down the road and found the seafood restaurant that a neighbor had recommended.

The soft-shell crab sandwich was delicious. It would have been delicious even if it had not been the only thing I had eaten that day except for the coffee and donuts that Mary had brought over that morning.

My God, I thought, is this still the same day.

Chapter 8

Change of Life

I awoke to sunshine streaming through the window, birds singing, noises from a campground in full swing and pain in every part of my body. I forced myself out of bed, carefully backing down the two, avocado green, carpeted stairs. A couple of unopened boxes took up half the space and I tried not to kick them. It took a special effort not to stumble on the bags and boxes that lay helter-skelter on the floor blocking much of the aisle. I managed the eight steps to the back of the trailer and into the bathroom without incident.

I washed my hands and face in the bathroom sink and discovered that the sink would have been better suited in a doll's house. I dried my face quickly and picked up my toothbrush and paste. I brushed my teeth in the kitchen sink. I dared not look around. I tried to stay focused on each task so I would not become overwhelmed.

I had traded fifteen hundred and ten square feet of condo space for twenty-two and a half linear feet on wheels and I could hardly move. I kept reminding myself that it had been my choice and I knew I would get used to it. I had to. This was home.

I removed my coffee maker from my tiny pantry and set it up on the cutting board that covered one half of my double sink. I found a coffee filter in the cupboard just above the counter. The coffee was located exactly where I had put it. It sat like a lonely sentinel in the nearly empty refrigerator waiting to be surrounded by tasty food stuffs. For the first time in years I had to use the water from my tap instead of a bottle because I had not had an opportunity to grocery shop. I measured two heaping spoons of coffee grounds and used my favorite blue mug, purchased in San Juan Capistrano, California years before to measure out two cups of water. My morning ritual was under way. I needed one cup to get my eyes open and another to get my heart started. I put my shorts and T-shirt on as the coffee dripped.

I had started my day like this was a normal day. I had no address except for two post office boxes.....one in Hawkesbury, Ontario, Canada and one in Sarasota, Florida. I had no home except for the one on wheels to be pulled by a super powerful diesel truck, the thought of which scared the hell out of me. I had left my friends and family to sit and wonder if I had lost my mind. This was not the usual 'change of life' that most fifty something year old women talk about. This was my change of life and every muscle in my body ached.

This was the beginning of my first day as a solo, full-time RVer.

Chapter 9

The First Day of the Rest of my Life

I lined the bottom of my cup with a couple of teaspoons of sugar before filling it with freshly brewed coffee. I sipped at it and discovered it tasted bitter without my usual healthy dose of milk.

I opened the door and pushed it all the way back to catch the hook. I then released the screen door. It clicked into place and I closed the little trap door to keep out flying intruders of all shapes and sizes and sporting any numbers of legs so prevalent in these climes.

I put the cup down on the picnic table that had been placed under my awning sometime that morning and removed the deck chair from under the trailer. I wiped it off with a towel to make sure that ants had not taken up residence before sitting down and retrieving my coffee cup. One more sip and I knew that I couldn't stand the coffee that way.

My neighbor, parked directly across the well-worn dirt path, had just come out of her thirty-two foot Holiday Rambler and sat down with a steaming cup of something. She looked my way and smiled. I extricated myself from the chair, feeling every muscle object, and sauntered over.

"Care for a shot of whiskey in that coffee," she asked as I approached.

"Sure," I responded, "it's after nine o'clock in the morning, isn't it? Actually if you have a little milk I would really appreciate it. I can't drink it black the way I feel."

"Sit," she said, "I'll get it for you."

It took only a minute or so for Marie to return. "You have no idea how sorry we felt for you yesterday," she volunteered.

"No sorrier than I felt for myself," I responded. "What an awful day it was. I had no idea I would have to unpack the truck myself and THEN have to put everything away so I could sleep in my bed. I'm taking a break today. The only thing I'll do today is get some groceries."

My neighbors were Dean and Marie Stratton from Gaylord, Michigan. They were my introduction to the wonderful people I would meet in my travels. Over the course of the next few days Marie and I talked our hearts out. We laughed a lot and cried a little. They learned my story and I listened to their heartbreaker.

Dean and his brother ran the family hardware business. He left the store one lunch hour to pick up a part for his car. He saw the truck heading for him. He even recognized the driver as a customer of his and was sure the man was playing a joke and would swerve at the last minute. Unfortunately, old and with poor eyesight, the customer had not seen Dean. In that split second in 1994 Dean and Marie's life, as they knew and loved, was over. For five weeks he lingered in a coma. To everyone's delight and shock, including the doctors who said he didn't have a chance, he opened his eyes one day and said to his son "what happened to me?" Life started over.

For most of that year and the next Marie was his nurse, slowing bringing him back from the brink of death. Dean suffered nerve damage, respiratory damage, brain damage and was left with an inability to swallow. As we talked, Dean spit. Before I knew about the accident, I was very uncomfortable with what I thought was a bad habit. After I knew, it didn't seem to be a problem. He however was very self-conscious and preferred eating by himself so no one had to watch. What remained in tact was his terrific sense of humor. He knew every joke going and brought them up at the most appropriate times. Marie was a godsend. She was friendly and patient and most helpful and never lost her sense of humor either. It was a hard lesson, but she now knows what is important in life. For my short time there I became part of that life.

My days in St. Augustine were filled with minor successes and major frustrations. I unpacked a couple of boxes whenever my energy allowed. The boxes going into

39

storage in Michigan left me so little room to maneuver I was cursing and swearing every time I turned around. I had to stop before I drove myself crazy which, at this point, would have been an extremely short trip.

One afternoon I toured what most people refer to as 'the oldest city in America' and discovered a commercial hodgepodge. I loved walking along the path near the water to the old fort and enjoyed a visit through Flagler College formerly the Ponce de Leon Hotel. The old homes and places of business turned tourist trap left me unimpressed. I wandered in and out of every business anyway just to say I did it. When I returned to the campground I put on my bathing suit and joined others in the hot tub and then the swimming pool. The hot tub worked its magic.

At some point each afternoon Marie and I imbibed in a cool libation. My spree at the supermarket had included the wine and spirits aisle for the first time in a long time. I bought the biggest bottle of White Zinfandel I could find and since it was too large and awkward to fit into my tiny refrigerator we needed ice cubes for chilling purposes. Without much effort we always finished the glass of wine before the cube, provided by Marie, melted.

"You know," Marie said on the third day of our afternoon ritual, "that really is a beautiful truck. You'll have no problem attracting the guys with that baby. All you have to do is lift the hood and put your finger to your cheek and the guys will come arunning." With that she put her index finger to cheek, lifted her eyebrows and gave me that sad puppy what-do-I-do-next look.

"You're right," I said, "that's why I call it my SSM.....super stud magnet."

We both erupted with laughter.

The afternoons with Dean and Marie were the highlight of my day.

Since this was still Florida and midnight hits around nine at night in this part of the world I found my evenings were either spent watching television in my camper, playing darts or working on puzzles in the community room.

It was in the morning on Saturday, April 4, 1998 that the real change came in my life.

Chapter 10

Lesson Number One.....and Only

I had not slept well. I was jittery and with good cause. I climbed out of bed before the sun was up and brewed my usual two cups of coffee. What little I tried to eat didn't sit well. I stopped trying.

I washed the dishes and put them in the cupboard. I placed many of the boxes on the floor and wedged them tightly so they would not slip and slide around on the drive. I stuffed pillows into all the cupboards that had anything in them that could break and stuffed the remaining pillows around my little twelve inch black-and-white television set that I had put on the floor and surrounded with boxes. I went to the office as soon as it opened and paid for the three extra nights that I had stayed. The first two nights had been included in my purchase package.

While I was at the office a couple of henchmen arrived at my trailer. By the time I returned, the water hose had been disconnected and put into a side cubbyhole. The sewer hose had been detached, cleaned and put into another cubbyhole designed specifically for it. The electricity had been unplugged and some little internal housing had sucked it up into itself. I arrived just as they were threading up the stabilizers with the crank used only for that purpose. Another handle was removed from God-knows-where and they were jacking up the front end of my trailer.

"Okay," said Donnie, "back up your truck. We'll guide you."

And guide me they did until the whole process got on their nerves and mine. I pulled forward a yard and backed up until I was a few inches off kilter then pulled forward and backed up again and again until I was sure that there was no way in hell I was ever going to be able to do this.

To add to the misery of this attempt I had not able to practice by myself since someone had to be there to close the tailgate before it slammed into the trailer. In my attempt at making sure that I had lots of pulling power for the trailer I had purchased, I discovered that I had enough power to pull a mansion and was, in actual fact, pulling an outhouse.....single-holer no less.

Glory be! On one of those backing up occasions I heard a loud crack of metal and discovered to my amazement that I had hit the bullseye.

"That's the sound ya need ta hear each time ya hook up," Fred the assistant, advised.

Donnie tried to plug in the trailer brakes, conveniently located a short crawling distance under the truck and discovered the cable wasn't long enough. He did the honor of pulling the trailer around the campground and parked it outside the workshop. He connected a longer cable wire, parked me behind the wheel, and we headed out onto the streets of highway A1A.

"Go way out onto the road before you turn right," said Donnie. "Right turns need a wide swing, remember that," came the voice from the passenger seat. "First road, turn right again," he said.

In preparation for the first right turn I applied the brakes. Fortunately the seat belt and a well-positioned steering wheel stopped me from having to be scraped off the windshield.

"Good," said Donnie, "the trailer brakes are working. Apply them a little lighter next time."

"Are they supposed to grab like that?" I asked totally astounded.

"How else are you going to stop the trailer?" came the winning response making me feel stupid for even having asked.

I pulled down the side road and was told to stop just past the first street. I won't go into minute detail about my learning to back up the monstrosity; however, with fifteen minutes of total frustration under my belt and never getting close to learning anything resembling backing up, I was told to drive around the block.

"When you get to a campground," advised my kindly and patient driving instructor, "ask for a pull-thru."

We drove around the block. I pulled back into the service center of the campground where my tires were filled with a little more air. Donnie backed the trailer out of the service entrance. He wished me luck, shook my hand and I was sent on my way. White knuckled, knees knocking and teeth chattering, I went out into the world of solo RVing.

This would be as good a time as ever for you to go back and reread chapter 3 where the salesman promised lessons, several days of free camping in their own campground in St. Augustine and I WOULD NOT BE ALLOWED ON THE ROAD UNTIL I WAS COMFORTABLE PULLING. As it turned out I was comfortable pulling. Stopping, turning and backing up however was another matter entirely.

I slowly made my way north on A1A until a paved side road sign pointed the way to Interstate 95. Once on this major highway, fortunately with little traffic, I was able to leave a county or two between me and whatever vehicle was in front of me, so frightened was I of having to make a quick stop. From Interstate 95 I maneuvered to Interstate 295 around Jacksonville, heaven forbid having to get close to a major city. From that highway it was an easy entrance onto Interstate 10 which connected with Interstate 75. I headed north on 75. Doesn't that sound easy.

Had I been in my car the whole trip would have been two and a half or three hours of relaxation and enjoyment, listening to country and western music all the way. However, I was driving an unfamiliar Ford F-250 powerstroke diesel truck, so loud that I couldn't hear the music over the sound of the engine and the pounding in my ears and pulling twenty-two and a half feet of home with everything I owned in the world riding inside.....that I couldn't stop and/or back up.

Doesn't it give you a certain amount of terror knowing that there are people like me on the road? Yup, that idea scares me too.

Well, to ease some of my tension, I pulled into every rest area on each of the highways. I checked my Trailer Life camping book at one of the stops and pulled out the name of the campground that I wanted to stay in when I reached Valdosta, Georgia. My total day's journey was one hundred and fifty-seven miles and took close to five hours.

The angels were riding on my shoulders that day. I got off the highway at the right exit. I turned the correct way for the campground that I wanted, swinging wide enough to clear the island in the middle of the road. The entrance was clearly visible as I approached and I was able to glide to a stop......and they had a pull-thru.

I paid for four days, pulled into my spot, released the rear stabilizers on the trailer and realized I had no idea what to do next.

Chapter 11

So Far So Good

I plugged in the electricity, connected the water and the sewer hoses and looked around in frustration. It was a little after three o'clock in the afternoon and there was just a few trailers parked intermittently. There were even fewer people. I sauntered up the aisle my home was on and every trailer in that row and the row opposite appeared vacant. Wandering down the third aisle, I was delighted to see a maroon red Ford F-350 all fancied up with dome lights and chrome steps into the cab and more importantly, a fifth wheel housing in the bed of the truck. As I rounded the corner onto the passageway, I spotted a threesome sitting under the awning and talking.

Without being a good judge of age, I assumed the woman facing me was in her fifties. She was blond, very pleasant looking, a little on the plump side wearing black shorts and a flowered, short-sleeved blouse. Even sitting on the picnic table I could see that she was considerably shorter than my five feet nine inches.

He too was shorter than I and looked so comfortable stretched out on a deck chair with his hands clasped behind his dark, wavy hair. The third, a woman, wearing jeans sat with her back to me and I could tell nothing about her.

Since there seemed to be an intense conversation going on I stopped and waited on the sidewalk until I was noticed. His hands were still clasped behind his head when he looked my way. "What can I do for you, Darlin?" he asked in a soft southern drawl.

"I have just pulled a fifth wheel trailer for the first time," I said rather timidly, "could you please watch me unhitch it to make sure that I'm doing it right?" I asked.

"Oh, Darlin," he said forcefully, "I can do better than that."

As we walked back to the first aisle, I thanked him for his help and suggested that, since he insisted on handling it all, he do one side and I do the other. "I really have to learn this," I said more confidently.

The first thing he did was thread up the rear stabilizers that I had released with a gentle reminder that they go down last. "If you put them down first you will break them off when you raise up the front of the trailer, or worse, they might crack the back of the trailer." "So, they go down last," he repeated softly.

The entire process, with an expert at the helm, took less than ten minutes with my knight in shining armor doing one side and my following the instructions for the other side. At some point, close to the end of the relatively simple operation, I unhitched my truck from the trailer.

I thanked him with a smile and a handshake. He left. I went into my trailer. I busied myself putting some of the boxes back up on the bunk beds, out of the way. The spice bottles were put out beside the stove. I would need them in preparation for cooking dinner. I checked the cupboards to see what I would make. I continued to fidget, not really knowing what to do with myself since it was still very early in the day. I found my book and tried reading. I took my computer and printer out of their hiding place and put them on the table hoping that I might get some work done. Everything I did to keep busy tore at my heart. I was alone in a trailer, not yet home, in a strange town. I couldn't stand it.

I took the remaining half bottle of white wine out of the refrigerator and went back to aisle three. The blond, giving me a warm smile introduced herself as Betty Deason and pointed to her husband, introducing him as Richard. "This is our friend and neighbor Jean Autry," she said. "That's her real name," she said with a smile not waiting for me to ask. "We've been talking about you, glad you came back. How come this is the first time you're unhitching. Sit," she said. "Tell us your story. You can't be traveling alone?" she asked absolutely astonished at the very idea.

I started by offering a drink from the bottle I was still holding.   Betty and Jean declined.   Pouring a drink for Richard and one for myself, I put the bottle on the table and took the chair that was offered.   The ladies seemed to be enjoying the beer they were drinking and Betty started asking questions as soon as I sat down.   It didn't take me long to tell them my story and it didn't take Betty long to invite me to stay for dinner.

"No, thank you," I said, "I really couldn't intrude."

"You're not intruding, we have enough food to feed everyone in the campground tonight," she said.   "Have you ever had a Cajun shrimp boil?"

"No," I answered enthusiastically, "but I love shrimp."

"We have six or seven pounds of shrimp, a couple dozen ears of corn and enough red-skinned potatoes to feed Georgia.   Jean's husband Tom will be home from work soon and we're just about ready to start," she volunteered.

Our friendship was cemented long before the picnic started.

Tom was the only fly in the ointment.   He looked slender in his jeans and cowboy boots with just a hint of a beer belly.   He was tall and dark with large, square glasses that covered much of his face.   The glasses made him look intelligent.   If he was it was masked by his redneck talk.   I don't quite know how he managed it but he seemed to disagree with everything and everyone even if we all had different opinions.

Dinner was started and served fairly early.   It was in a giant black pot, supported by a tripod, that gallons of water and the Cajun spices were set to boiling.   The two-bite red potatoes went in first.   Fifteen or twenty minutes later, after a few potatoes were pricked with a fork to test doneness, the ears of corn that had been halved followed their food mates into the cauldron. With just a few minutes remaining, a basket of king-sized, white beauties were thrown into the rolling boiling pot.   Everything was coated in the red spice, hot enough to need some getting used to, but that chore didn't take long. Within minutes the bottom half of my face and mouth were numb.

Retrieved from its hiding place, under their thirty-five foot fifth wheel trailer, were two chests filled with ice that covered soft drinks, several varieties of beer and a couple of large bottles of wine. My meager contribution was long gone.

The table lacked eating utensils. A slotted spoon scooped dinner out of the pot into a covered ceramic dish. We had to help ourselves from there. A giant ladle helped fill our plates. From there it became finger foods. The potatoes and corn were picked up and rolled in dishes of artery-clogging butter, one dish placed at each end of the picnic table. The shrimp had to be peeled before being eaten. We ate and drank, occasionally making an effort to wipe our hands and faces. I was not the only one that had butter dripping off the end of their chin. The conversation never stopped.

As tough a day as it had been, what a glorious way for it to end. Since Richard had to be at work at six in the morning and Betty had to get him there because she needed the truck to get to work at Wal-Mart, it was all over by nine in the evening. When I said good night after clean up Betty said, "we'll expect you here tomorrow at five, we're having brisket on the barbecue." There was no way I could refuse and why on God's green earth would I want to anyway.

The four days in Valdosta, Georgia were filled with new and enjoyable experiences. As a Toastmaster, I visited a group in that city. Although the session was to start at six forty-five in the morning, I chose the first Monday after the time had changed to attend a meeting. That was definitely a mistake. Normally there would have been twenty or more in the group, I was told. Only five others dragged themselves out at that ungodly hour. The president asked, giving me the evil eye if I dared to refuse, if I would like to give the Icebreaker speech. That first speech in the beginners manual is a way of introducing yourself, formally, to the group. Since I am a CTM (meaning Competent Toastmaster, having successfully completed the first ten speeches) and without a speech from me the meeting would have been over in fifteen minutes instead of an hour and a half, I gladly accepted. I loved the experience.

I also spent an afternoon shopping, something I rarely do and almost never enjoy. I purchased a couple of Neil Diamond CD's. My truck came equipped with a CD player and since it was my first one, my listening collection needed expanding.

I also shopped for a special chocolate cake dessert to bring to the barbecued brisket dinner and a large bottle of Apelia Red found its way into my cart. I also needed a few extra groceries since I had decided to invite Richard and Betty, Jean and Tom to a special Beef Stew dinner.....special because of the French spice, Herbs de Province that I added to the recipe.

The reason for the four day stay in Valdosta was a lecture I would be doing at Books-A-Million. I awoke on April 8, exactly one year to the day that my book Restless From The Start was published, to a rainstorm like no other. It was an excellent test for the rubber roof and the seals around the windows in my trailer. Fortunately nothing leaked but the solid sheets of ice cold water, with winds up to twenty or thirty miles an hour, made for a lousy day. I couldn't stand being locked up all day so I bundled up in my yellow slicker made for occasions such as this and found my golf umbrella. The bookstore was a great place to kill a few hours. There was another author there that afternoon but the store was almost empty. I stayed for a couple of hours hoping that someone would do the same for me that evening. I went home late afternoon, had dinner, changed clothes and was back at the bookstore at seven that night. The deluge never let up. I read excerpts from my book to the few people who were there and thankfully Richard and Betty came in for half an hour to keep me company.

The Deasons waited up for me that evening. I returned a little after nine. In the rain, Richard helped me hook up my truck and trailer, afraid that there would be no one there in the morning to help. I kissed them both good night and goodbye and promised to stay in touch.

It was a wonderful way to end my first solo camping experience.

Chapter 12

Nasty Business

I awoke early. I made some coffee that, once again, didn't sit well in my stomach. I washed all the dishes and stacked them in the cupboard. I put things where I knew they would be secure mainly on the floor and surrounded by pillows. I again stuffed the rest of the pillows into the dish cupboard and the pantry where my coffee maker was kept. My packing up method was becoming a ritual.

I went out into a day that was dark and overcast. The storms of the night before had abated but the ground was spongy and puddles had formed on the pavement just outside my door. There was no way to side step the pool without landing in the muck and mire of the grass. I returned to the trailer to put on my sandals since I preferred driving in my sneakers and didn't want to get them wet.

I unplugged the electricity and disconnected the water and sewer. I was not more than half way through the process when tears welled up in my eyes and it became necessary to stop for a minute. It just seemed like so much work for one person.

"If Paul were here," I mumbled under my breath, "he would do the outside and I could do the inside like we always did in Europe."

Feeling sorry for myself rarely lasted long. As a matter of fact it usually only lasted the length of time that a nasty job had to be done.....and disconnecting and cleaning a sewer hose, trust me, is a nasty job. I cranked up the back and front stabilizers. Thanks to Richard the trailer was already attached to my truck. I took a minute to walk the truck and trailer perimeter making sure all the little cubbyholes were locked, the windows were closed and the vents down in preparation for getting on the road. I also checked the hitch, that we had connected in the dark, was closed and bolted into place.

While the truck warmed up I said a silent prayer to the little brass angel that is clipped onto the sun visor, given to me as a gift at the closing of my condo by my real estate agent. I loved the little angel, however, every time I touched it, I was reminded of the prayer said by some comedian.....when I die, I want it to be like my grandfather, who died peacefully in his sleep.....not like the passengers in the back seat of his car, kicking and punching and screaming. Even under tension that joke always produced a smile.

It was around ten o'clock when I pulled out into the real world. I was close to the highway and had no trouble finding the entrance. The workers were at work. The buses had delivered the children to school and were already off the road. There was not much traffic. This was another day that I wouldn't be traveling far, approximately one hundred and fifty miles by my map to Byron, Georgia just south of Macon.

Again I stopped at every rest area and discovered that my little home, as uncomfortable as I was pulling it around, seemed to be following me like a bloodhound on the scent of beef jerky that was dangling from a stick taped to his collar. At one stop I made sure that the little wire dangling from a metal box on the side of the fifth wheel arm was attached separately and securely as it was supposed to be. Should this bloodhound lose the scent of the beef jerky and decide to head off in another direction this wire would pull on its automatic breaking system and would stop the runaway trailer. Or so I'd been told.

It boggled my mind the number of important things that I had to worry about while I was out there on the road.....alone.

At one of the rest stops a Buddy Gregg, one of those seven hundred and fifty thousand dollars motorhomes pulled up beside me, dwarfing mine. A youngish couple, a single older woman and a brace of golden retrievers got out about the same time I got out. The older woman immediately approached.

"My God," she said, "you're not driving that thing alone, are you?"

53

I instantly perked up and said, "yes, I am." In that moment I felt particularly proud and brave.

She asked a lot of questions and when I told her that I was a writer and doing a bit of a book tour she asked to see my book. She purchased an autographed copy, handed me her card and explained that she owned a bookstore and was always on the lookout for unique things. "If you get to Dahlonega, Georgia," she said, "you'll do a book signing in my store."

I thanked her and promised that I would drop in if I ever got up to her neck of the woods. I went on my way feeling very pleased with myself.

At the next rest area I checked the Trailer Life camping book and chose a campground close to the highway and thankfully, once again, had no trouble finding the turnoff for it. I pulled in, went up to the office and discovered a sign on the door that said, "Pay Next Door at the Garage. Back at 3:00 P.M."

I paid, picked out a level stop and pulled my trailer into it. I plugged in the electricity, hooked up the water and sewer and stopped. I did not want to take a chance doing it all myself. I still needed someone to watch me. No one was about.

I bought a Macon newspaper and settled down on my deck chair to wait for someone from the office to return. What a delightful surprise awaited me on page two of the paper.

Chapter 13

And Handsome To Boot

There it was on page two under specials events in the Macon area, Joei Carlton Hossack would be lecturing on her travels to Alaska at Books-A-Million. A stranger in a strange land and my name, familiar only to me, pops up on the pages of the local newspaper. I loved it.

Another shocker awaited me on those printed pages. While I had complained bitterly about the rainstorm that I had endured in Valdosta, tornado after tornado had touched down devastating parts of Alabama, Mississippi and Georgia. Thirty-eight people had died in Birmingham, two in rural Mississippi and many more in Atlanta, a terrifyingly short distance from Valdosta. The devastation to property had totaled in the millions. The devastation to people's lives could only be calculated in tears. I read and reread in stunned silence.

It was around three in the afternoon that the office opened. Suddenly the whole campground was alive with activity. Motorhomes were waiting in line to get into the park. The camp itself was a rather scruffy looking place with earth where grass should have been growing and a road around and through the park that was desperately in need of grading or paving or both but it was the closest one to Macon. Long before dark it became a popular overnight stop.

He was a rather handsome man by my standards. He had dark wavy hair touched with a hint of gray at the temples. He appeared to be fifty something years old and solidly built. He sauntered over. "Did you need some help?" he asked not mincing words. "They sent me from the office."

"Thank you, yes," I replied. "I really don't know how to unhitch this thing yet. I'll do it, you just instruct."

Even with my doing all the work, the entire process didn't take long and Ken White, the campground host, as he introduced himself, opened the tailgate as I pulled out from under it.

He didn't wait around. There were suddenly more campers waiting in line. Each camper had to be escorted to a spot and Ken lead the way in a golf cart. In a couple of hours the campground was filled to capacity with transients most staying only one night.

By early evening I was wandering around and checking license plates. Most campers were too busy to talk. People were hooking up, puttering indoors, cooking dinner outdoors, lighting barbecues or carrying baskets loaded with dirty clothes to the laundry room. No one appeared to be traveling solo. Although most nodded or smiled politely there was no one who made an effort to chat. I retired early.

The date was Friday, the tenth of April. My husband Paul and I should have been celebrating our twenty second wedding anniversary but here I was trying to keep myself busy until five o'clock when I would be heading out to find Books-A-Million in Macon. I wandered into the campground office needing to know where I could find a large grocery store in Byron. In addition to the grocery store information I learned that the motorhome parked three sites away from mine had motor problems. I retrieved my purse from the trailer and went over to the disabled vehicle. I knocked on their door. It was answered by an older woman well into her sixties possibly seventies.

"I understand that you're having some problems with your motorhome. I'm going to the grocery store. Is there anything you need?" I asked.

"Come on in," she said, obviously grateful for the intrusion.

"How nice of you," she said. "My name is Maxine and this is my husband, Shannon."

I turned to face him as he came into the living room from the back of their motorhome. I hoped that my face didn't register the shock I felt. I was looking into the cherubic face of a young man in his early thirties. Had I heard correctly? Did she say husband.

"Yes," she repeated, "Shannon is my husband." "We've been married a little over five years." "Are you shocked?" she asked.

"Well, if it were the other way around," I babbled, "no one would dare say anything. Do people comment?" I asked, never really answering her question.

"They did at first, but not so much in our home town anymore," Maxine volunteered. "Would you care for some coffee or tea?" she asked.

"Thanks, but I really need to get some groceries. Can I take a raincheck?" I asked.

I roamed around the easily forgettable town of Byron before I found a reasonably large, poorly stocked, rather dark and dingy looking grocery store. I picked up a few necessities and headed back towards the campground. I wasn't fussy about the area I was in and there didn't seem to be much beyond the so-called supermarket except for open fields and farmhouses in the distance. With the groceries, all non-perishable, sitting on the floor by the passenger seat, I stopped at a Starvin Marvin for fuel. I pulled into the bay, filled my tank and noticed that each bay had long-handled brushes, large sponges and buckets for washing vehicles. When I paid for the fuel I asked what it would cost to wash my truck.

"Be my guest," he said as he handed me back the change from a twenty.

This was a real treat since most campgrounds did not allow washing vehicles of any sort. I threw myself into the task. I rolled up my pant legs, turned the nozzle on full blast, flinching as the spray tickled my face. I hosed down the truck from headlights to taillights, concentrating on some of the hard packed muddy areas at the bottom of the doors. I took out one of the big brushes, dipped it into the soapy solution and started cleaning. I must have looked like I was enjoying the task because an older man approached, smiling at me.

"When they find out that more women than men own these monster trucks are they going to take away these goodies?" I asked.

"Nice rig," he said giving me the thumbs up sign. He walked past and into the store looking back only once.

I was back at the campground in time to make myself a light dinner and shower. I changed my clothes and headed into Macon for my duties at the bookstore. I had left myself too much time fearing that I would get lost en route. Not a chance. The manager at the Valdosta store had given me directions and they were perfect. The store was less than a mile off the highway exit. I had over an hour to kill. I wandered around the store, then the strip shopping mall and then back into the bookstore as the sun went down, too chilly to stay outside.

For my lecture on Alaska two interested women listened. We turned it into an informal discussion over coffee since they had not seen the ad in the paper and were there just to browse. I told them about Alaska and Betty Bass and Maria Ryne told me about Macon and their lives. I was home by nine, satisfied, not necessarily with book sales but with my new sense of freedom. I was definitely finding my way around even in strange southern towns.

Saturday was my day off. I read awhile. I wandered the campground hoping to find a friendly face or two. I walked out to the main road where an ice cream shop showed signs of life. When a truck pulling a fifth wheel trailer pulled into the station for gas, I stopped to talk to the driver, taking the occasional lick from my cone.

"When you put your foot on the brake," I asked innocently, "does everything slam to a stop."

"No," he answered.

"Mine does," I said.

"Oh my God," he said, "didn't anyone show you how to adjust your trailer brakes."

"No," I answered.

We only talked a few minutes but I picked up a few tips about the brakes before I left. I thanked him for the information. The pralines and cream ice cream cone was delicious and feeling much better about the situation, I relaxed on an outside bench before heading back to the campground to finish reading my book.

That was where Ken found me. I was sitting on my lawn chair, under the extended awning, reading my book when he approached. I had been right that first glance, he really was rather good looking. He certainly was better looking than anyone I had seen in Florida. To add to his charm he was soft spoken and without much of the southern drawl that took forever to complete a sentence. Since I had just made myself a cup of tea I asked him to join me. I was surprised when he accepted.

Early afternoons for him were slow so we talked of little things like tea and good camping spots and favorite eating places and gas stations supplying hoses and sponges for washing. We talked about big things like my struggle with widowhood and his struggle with divorce.

"Where did the afternoon go," he asked when he looked up and saw a string of motorhomes waiting to be escorted to their spots. "Gotta go," he said.

He returned around eight and invited me to join him for steak on the barbecue. Unfortunately I had eaten at least an hour before knowing that he would be busy for most of the evening. "I'll have a glass of wine while you have your dinner," I offered.

"I'd rather have a hot dog with a friend," he said, "than eat steak by myself."

We rode around the campground in his golf cart. We stopped and talked to some of the permanent residents who had planted gardens. In between visits we talked quietly. He never did have dinner.

It had been quite a day. From my point of view Florida had been devoid of eligible men in my age group. Things were looking up. They were definitely looking up.

"Do you really have to leave tomorrow?" he asked.

Chapter 14

A Necessary Adjustment

The sun was not quite up when I awoke. I got out of bed and immediately started packing up while the coffee brewed. By the time I opened the door the inside work was almost completed. Ken was talking to a local resident parked directly across from me. He came over as soon as he saw me.

"I have coffee for you," he said. He returned to his trailer as soon as I told him how I liked it prepared. He was back in no time.

"Are you sure you really have to go today?" he repeated himself from the night before.

"If I were really confident pulling my trailer," I responded, "I would wait a couple of days but the thought of driving through Atlanta on any day but a Sunday scares the hell out of me." He seemed to agree but was genuinely upset at my leaving. I certainly would have enjoyed a few more days in that campground.

"Let's hitch you up," he said, "and drive around a bit."

Having just plugged in the trailer brakes he parked himself behind the wheel of my truck. He gently put his foot down on the brake pedal as his fingers reached for a little switch on the black box that had been attached under my dash board and glowed red every time I stepped on the brake whether the trailer was attached or not.

"See this lever," he said lifting his hand away from the box, "slide it across slowly. That will stop the trailer manually. If your trailer ever starts to sway uncontrollably you can pull on the trailer brakes without stopping the truck. Don't look so worried," he said with a little grin, "fifth wheels don't sway much."

He reached down the side of the black box and moved a tiny panel forward. "This will adjust the trailer to stop with your truck brake. Reach down and slide it forward slowly," he said. As I moved the panel forward Ken stepped on the brake and we slowed and stopped gradually. "Okay, your turn behind the wheel," he said.

We changed places. I could feel nothing but relief as we drove around the campground again and again. I played with the knob and panel until I felt reasonably comfortable with the adjusted brake and thrilled that I now knew how to do it myself. We stopped at my site so we could have another cup of coffee.

"Do you really have to leave?" he asked again.

It was around ten in the morning when I pulled out of the front gate of the Interstate Campground and RV Center. As I approached Atlanta I started feeling queasy. I had driven through on several occasions but only by car and even then I had been somewhat intimidated. I vaguely remembered always having to pull into other lanes. As I approached there were signs that said "anything over six wheels must use I-285" and I ignored the signs assuming that it applied only to trucks.

There were no trucks and only a few cars on any of the highways leading in, around and through the city. Even though my heart was beating too loud for me to hear the music and my mouth too dry to produce any amount of spit, I managed without incident to make it through the city. It was a long drive before I found a rest area where I could unwind from the tension. I walked and walked and walked and gradually fell in line with another lady who was walking the rest area.

Feeling rather proud of myself I told her that I was pulling a fifth wheel trailer myself.

"How far are you going?" she asked.

"My nephew lives in Ann Arbor, Michigan so I'll be stopping there for a few days before going into Canada," I said. "I think my second book will be printed in Michigan," I added, "so I want to spend some time in the area."

"Oh," she said, having aroused her curiosity, "what do you write about?"

"I write travel," I answered.

"Have you ever been on an Elderhostel?" she asked.

"No, I'm not old enough," I responded.

"Oh, sure you are," she said. "They're wonderful, you should go."

"I'm not old enough," I said again.

"Oh, sure you are," she said. "My husband and I went on one teaching jazz." "They not only give you the history but they play music and tell you about each artist. It is really a wonderful experience. You should go," she said.

"I'm not old enough," I responded.

"Oh, sure you are," she said. "They don't always have the greatest of accommodations but the learning aspect is wonderful." "You should try it," she said.

"I'm not old enough," I said.

"Oh, sure you are," she said just as her husband arrived.

"This lady is a travel writer," she said to her husband, "and I'm trying to convince her to go on an Elderhostel."

"Oh, the one we were on was terrific," he said, "you should go."

"I'm not old enough," I said.

"How old do you have to be to go on an Elderhostel?" she asked her husband.

"Fifty-five, I think," he answered.

"Yes," I responded, "you have to be fifty-five." "I'm not old enough," I said.

"Oh, sure you.......we've got to go," she said and they rushed off to their car never looking back.

I snickered to myself as I walked back to my truck. "I really must get rid of this gray hair," I said to myself. "I know I would look a hell of a lot younger."

Chapter 15

Always Learning Something

I drove too far that day. I was so thrilled with having made it through Atlanta without problems and had enjoyed the embarrassing antics at the rest stop that I just continued driving well beyond what was comfortable for me. I ended that day in Athens, Tennessee two hundred and fifty-eight miles from where I started that morning in Byron, Georgia.

The stocky, balding little guy in jeans and a Tennessee T-shirt spouting a British accent checked me in. We spent a little time talking about his former home in Bath, England, a familiar part of the world and an area that I loved dearly. He had been in Tennessee over twenty years, after a stint in Chicago, and still sounded like a displaced person but he loved Tennessee "where everyone had time to talk awhile."

"Why are you selling, then?" I asked letting him know that I had seen the For Sale sign at the entrance of the campground.

"I put the sign up right after I bought the place," he said. "You never know who might be interested in an investment. I could make a killing without doing anything," he said. "If it sells, it sells. I'll always find something else to do," he confided.

"Okay, where would you like me to park?" I asked.

"We'll talk again when I'm settled."

All the sites thankfully were pull-thrus and I drove around the perimeter until I found my spot. It took about fifteen minutes to attach all the hoses and things. Inside I set up the television set and computer and took all the pillows out of the cupboards and threw them up onto the bed. As soon as I sat on the bed and flipped on the television set the now familiar wiggly line shimmered in front of my eyes. I dampened a washcloth with cold water, put a couple of ice cubes in the middle of it, covered my eyes and lay back down on my bed. It was the start of another "classic" migraine that

I managed to avert. If there were flashing lights and black holes I didn't know about them. I closed my eyes and must have dozed a bit because by the time I got up, I felt fine. I vowed not to drive that far again.

I kept a low profile that evening leaving the camper only long enough to call Mary using the ten dollar calling card I had purchased in St. Augustine. We didn't talk long, a few minutes, but long enough to know that I was missed.

After the call I walked around to the front of the building. The office was closed and my little English friend was nowhere to be found. I returned to the camper and spent that evening watching television.

By the time I was ready to leave the next morning the campground was empty of overnighters. The office was closed with a note on the door that said they would be open at five. I had to knock on a few doors that showed signs of life for someone to come help by closing the tailgate as I backed up. It was a young woman that volunteered assistance and I apologized for taking her away from her children. Her husband was asleep. "He works all night," she said and although her children were old enough to be left alone for short periods of time she feared a squabble that would break out if she were gone too long and awaken 'Sleeping Beauty.' Her words, not mine.

It was a simple task and took only minutes. She seemed to want to talk awhile but, since it was after eleven o'clock, I was now anxious to be on my way. We talked only a few minutes. I thanked her and left.

It was a one hundred and fifty-eight mile drive to Corbin, Kentucky. The signs from the highway pointed the way to the KOA campground. The directions in my Trailer Life camping book said it was close to the highway, which I liked, but there were so many twists and turns that I became uncomfortable going down the narrow roads and bumpy lanes. When I finally came across the office and checked in I was not happy with the "woodsiness" of it all. Nothing was level. The sites were gravel and earth and hook ups were scattered all over the place. I stayed anyway. My next door neighbor, acknowledging my plight, loaned me a length of water hose that I could attach onto my short twenty-five foot length. Obviously he was much more acquainted with this natural type of setting and had extras and spares of everything. The campground office conveniently had extra hoses for sale but I would have had to mortgage my camper to purchase one.

Once parked I had trouble unhitching. The trailer was on relatively flat ground but my truck was on a sharp downhill grade. After much frustration my full-timing neighbor suggested that I back up a smidgen. Problem solved. The fifth wheel housing needed that tiny back up motion to release itself. If his wife had not been around I swear I would have kissed him.

We all, wife included, sat and enjoyed some small talk, a soft drink and a large bag of roasted peanuts in the shell. What we didn't eat we gave to the squirrels that came around begging. We soon had a crowd of the little critters running helter-skelter in all directions, each with a peanut in their cheek. They were not happy when we ran out of food for them.

With a few chores to do I didn't hang around long. I asked if they needed something from town or the grocery store if I found it. When they declined my offer I thanked them for their help and left.

Since my camel was now free from its hump I drove into Corbin, withdrew a couple of hundred dollars on my bank card, purchased enough groceries for a few days, filled up with diesel and returned to the campground just before dark. I was a little more confident knowing that even with all the twists and turns I would be able to find my way back to the highway the next day.

I tried calling my sister that night to wish her a happy birthday but she was not at home. It was a lonely evening with only two uninteresting and fuzzy channels coming in on my little twelve inch black-and- white set.

Chapter 16

Another Success

The minute I pulled that damn trailer across the road
I knew I was going in the wrong direction. "Please, please,
please let there be a place for me to turn around," I prayed
silently.

It had rained all night at my last stop and in the
morning a heavy dampness hung in the air. I waited for it to
stop completely and by eight-thirty was starting to do the
outside work. My neighbor had helped me hitch up. I
cleaned and wiped dry the water hose that I had borrowed
from him and returned it. At ten in the morning I was back
on the road as uncomfortable as ever but pleased that I was
making progress in the learning department.

As always I had studied the camping guide the
evening before and discovered several campgrounds that were
not too many twists and turns off the highway. Each
potential was written on a separate scrap of paper and taped,
in order of distance, to the dashboard of my truck. On route I
stopped at every rest area between Corbin and Walton, my
last potential, and was delighted to have made it around
another big city, Lexington, Kentucky without incident.

I had gotten off at the correct exit and as soon as I
had pulled my trailer into the middle of the first juncture, too
late to change directions, I realized that I was supposed to
turn left. I was heading west. I had written southwest. I
could easily have pulled into the Flying J gas station on my
left but I was so rattled by my mistake that I missed the
entrance completely. Even though the station covered the
entire street corner I drove right by the side entrance. With
only one mile left to travel to the safety and security of the
campground I was lost on a very narrow, two-lane country
road wandering around in the hills, fifteen miles south of
Cincinnati.

"Please, please, please let there be some large circular driveway for me to turn around," I prayed. I looked up at each farmhouse on either side as I drove. There was nothing.

I was at least five miles down the road when a dark blue pickup truck headed towards me. I pulled over to the side and stopped. I rolled down my window and waved my arm hoping the young man behind the wheel would stop.

"What can I do for ya, Ma'am?" he asked.

"I missed the turnoff to the campground," I answered, "will there be a place for me to turn around up the road?"

"No Ma'am," he responded, "but if you go down to the end of the road and turn left you'll get to it that way."

"How far down to the end of the road?" I asked.

"It's about seven miles to the end of this road and about five miles after you turn left. Be real careful," he said, "there's a big garbage truck a mile or two down the road."

I waved my hand and thanked him. I sat still for a moment trying to breathe easily and relax. I was horrified. One little slip up and it had cost me dearly.....seventeen endless miles and unbelievable stress.

The young man had told the truth. I hadn't gone far when the garbage truck loomed up in front of me blocking almost the entire road. I pulled over to the side getting as close to the ditch as I dared. There was no way I was going around him. He was going around me. As he pulled closer I rolled down my window.

"I missed the turnoff to the campground," I said. "Will there be a driveway or something that I can turn around in."

"No," he responded, "but if you go to the end of this road and turn left it's about five miles on your left. Be careful with the turn," he said, "it's real sharp.

I was relieved that the young man had been honest with me and I drove slowly up and down the hills before coming to the end of the road. The left turn was a sharp one but not one that I could not manage. I was thrilled when I found the entrance into the campground and only slightly shaken when I asked for a pull-thru and she said "no."

"Sorry," came the reply, "we save those for motorhomes pulling cars."

"I've never backed up before," I said hoping she would see how shaken I was and relent.

"Don't worry," she answered, "I'll send my brother out to help you."

I paid for the camping spot adding fifteen dollars for a Good Sam Camping Club membership. I immediately saved a couple of bucks off the price of the camping. I drove down to the overnight area and parked waiting for someone.....anyone.....to come to my rescue.

An old beat up white Chevy truck, with more dents and rust spots on it than I could count on all my appendages, pulled into the spot beside me. The driver was as battered-looking as the truck but he seemed to know what he was doing. Thankfully, he had the patience of Job. It took over half an hour of pulling forward and backing the beast up before I was in and once parked my trailer was too off-kilter to stay that way.

My heavy set, greasy looking angel went to find some boards to put under the wheels on the left side of my trailer. I dreaded the repeat performance. I thought I would have to start all over again. The last part, however, was easy. I pulled forward, he put the boards down and I back it up straight. Despite the fact that I was worn out and frustrated from my earlier effort I was thrilled that I had actually done it. Since I would be leaving relatively early the next morning I didn't bother to unhitch.

I spent that evening talking to my next door neighbor who was putting the finishing touches on a hand-crocheted dress for an Indian Doll. I kept one eye on the handicraft work and the other on the campers that were just arriving, filling up the overnight spots. Despite my delight at backing up for the first time I would have been really pissed off if it had been for nothing. All the pull-thrus were occupied long before dark.

Before the night was over I called my sister again. I left a birthday message on her answering machine.

Chapter 17

I Need A Break

I didn't leave Oak Creek campground as early as I would have liked and for a most enjoyable reason. She was about my own age with dark hair, pale complexion and sparkling brown eyes. He was tall and slender with beautiful blue eyes hidden behind tortoise framed glasses. When they were meeting and greeting people in the various campgrounds they were thoroughly enjoying themselves. They were traveling, full-time, like myself. Illness had forced him to take early retirement but he delighted in volunteer work. Being Santa Claus at Christmas time was pure joy to him. He couldn't resist pulling out a bunch of pictures from the various nursing homes and hospitals where he had performed. I certainly would not have minded sitting on his lap and telling him what I wanted for Christmas.

They had seen me wandering around the evening before and were sure that I was traveling alone. They wanted to talk and I was delighted with the attention. So I left late.

Sharon, owner of the campground, had suggested that I take the bypass around Cincinnati since the city was a mess with construction. The highway was limited to one lane and even a flat tire on the route would spell hours of delay. She forgot to mention that they would not have let me go through the city anyway and that I had to take the bypass.

The route I had chosen, west around the city, was free from traffic but what a long, tedious road. The highway seemed to meander into Indiana before returning to Ohio. I drove over forty miles out of my way west and many miles north. Once back on Interstate 75, I stopped at the first rest area. I spoke to a middle-aged hippy, who did not seem to be aware that the nineteen sixties had been over for several decades, driving a Volkswagen van. He had taken the road through the city. "No problem," he said, "but it was one lane right through the city with cones and cement blocks keeping you in your lane."

I suddenly felt better for having taken the bypass. I would have been unnerved with cement blocks and one lane mile after mile. Frankly the whole trip was starting to unnerve me. I needed a break for a few days but unless I wanted to take up residence in a nearly empty campground it would be a few more days before I got one.

Again I had written out directions to several campgrounds from my Trailer Life and they were taped to my dashboard. As I approached Bluffton, Ohio I was more than ready to call it quits for the day. As I neared the exit I hoped for some sign that there was indeed an open campground. I needed an indication on the highway and there was none. As soon as I passed the exit I saw a lively looking campground on my right.

"Oh, hell, why didn't I take a chance," I scolded myself.

I even debated turning around at the next exit but adding even one extra mile onto an already too long journey was unthinkable. I just kept going. I stopped at the next rest area just to calm down a bit. It was loaded with big rigs. I pulled in beside one and got my camping book out again to make sure that the one in Van Buren was really open. According to the book the campground opened April fifteenth and the day was April fifteenth. The farther north I drove the more trouble I was having finding open places to stay so adding fear to an already uncomfortable situation did not help matters.

I suddenly became aware of a large fifth wheel and truck that was parked at the end of the row. The truck had its hood up. I felt sorry for the older couple standing by the disabled vehicle since I could all too easily imagine myself in that predicament. I did not approach since there was no way that I could be of any help. Besides with so many truckers around, I knew help, certainly better than I could provide, was within asking distance.

After checking the camping book one more time I started my engine prepared to take off. I had driven only a few feet when the old gentleman walked in front of my truck. I slammed on the brakes, causing the trailer to hiccup to a stop, and rolled down my window.

"Englais ou Francais?" he asked.

The question itself unnerved me since I had Florida plates on both truck and trailer. "English," I responded.

"I'm having problems with my truck," he said. "Do you know anything about transmissions?"

"No," I replied.

"Are you going into town?" he asked.

"No," I responded.

"Could you please drive me to the nearest town," he asked.

"I'm sorry, no," I replied forcefully now totally unnerved and suspicious. I couldn't get out of there fast enough. With all the truckers and other travelers at the rest area why had he chosen a gray-haired woman traveling alone to approach. I was convinced at the time, and am to this day, that those sweet little oldies were up to no good.

It was about a half-hour more of driving, approximately twenty-five miles north on Interstate 75, that I arrived in Van Buren, Ohio. The sign on the highway indicated the campground and more signs on the side roads made finding the campground a breeze even though it was a fair distance off the beaten path. Although not all the facilities were available, the campground was indeed open.

After paying, I pulled into one of the more level spots, turned off the motor and was immediately greeted by a friendly face. Beryl Sargant from Rhodesia started by inviting me into her motorhome for a cup of tea.

"I'd love it," I said. I plugged in the electricity and walked two sites away to her home.

I felt so grateful and relieved to be safely tucked away for the night and to be enjoying the company of another. She was tall and willowy-slender which was a look I always admired. High cheekbones on a very pretty face were surrounded by long, dark auburn hair. She was soft spoken when she talked about her family. She had three children, two in the United States and one son in England. She had several grandchildren and a set of twin boys both born with very severe birth defects. I listened to her grief, not saying much. She confided that the only thing that kept her and her husband going were their faith in God and how her belief made each day a joy. I nodded in agreement.

I think she took that as a sign to continue or perhaps she would have continued anyway. The more she talked about Jesus the more adamant she became. Becoming a little uncomfortable, I tried changing the subject on a couple of occasions. I also kept returning the pamphlets that she insisted upon giving me but it didn't work. Just about the time I was ready to cut and run, mentioning that I had better set up my camper, her husband arrived from work. I hoped he would rescue me.

Fortunately I didn't have to try very hard to get back to my camper. She and her husband, Ian, were going out to inspect some other campgrounds where they could set up permanent residence.

I thanked them for their hospitality. I wished them luck and we all left together.

Another fifth wheel pulled in late afternoon and we exchanged pleasantries. They were from Fenelon Falls, Ontario. Although I had not seen a bit of rain that day they had come through a horrendous rainstorm accompanied by large hailstones and were delighted to be safe for the night.

Knowing that the next day would be my last day traveling for a few days I slept reasonably well.

73

Chapter 18

Family Reunion

I had almost escaped. Everything inside was packed and road ready. The outside work was in its final stages when I spotted Beryl coming towards me, packet in hand. She wished me Godspeed and handed me the packet insisting I open it. I opened it, thanked her and returned it.

"Please give the information to someone who will appreciate it," I said, trying to hide my annoyance. "I'm Jewish," I reminded her for the fifth or sixth time, "and I'm planning on staying that way." I changed the subject by asking about the campground they had gone to visit the night before. She told me they would be moving at the end of the month.

She kissed me goodbye and I went back to removing and wiping hoses before putting them in their cubbyholes.

It was overcast when I drove out through the gates but the sun was really making an effort to come out. Within an hour on the highway it finally won and the day seemed almost perfect. My drive was supposed to be less than a hundred miles to Petersburg, Michigan. The KOA that I had chosen was less than a mile off the highway. That too seemed perfect. The camping book listed its official opening date as April fifteenth and it was now the sixteenth so I was confident that there would not be a problem. Just before the exit to the campground there was a rest area with a staffed information center. I don't know why but I decided to stop. The woman behind the counter that I was speaking with decided to call the campground just to make sure. My heart sunk. They would not be open until Friday.....the next day. I would have to look elsewhere.

She called the KOA in Ypsilanti. It was another twenty-five or thirty mile drive and right into heavy traffic but it was indeed open for business. They gave me step by step directions and I checked, rechecked and wrote out each turn and highway number in bold print, before getting on my way. If I had had any other choice, I would have taken it. I got back into my truck, knees knocking and gripping the steering wheel for dear life. Only once did I come close to being wiped out in the heavy traffic around Ann Arbor but once is more than enough. I was on highway 94 heading east and had to cross over a couple of lanes of traffic coming onto the highway. It all happened so fast. I had to get over to the slow lane to get off the highway at the upcoming exit. The car, seeing my flashing signal light to pull over, took special pains to speed up. I was forced to slow to a crawl while still in the fast lane to let him pass. The car behind the jerk, realizing my dilemma, backed off to let me enter the slow lane. I was very relieved, and only slightly shaken, when I got off the highway. I followed the directions from the camping book. When I pulled into the campground I wanted to kiss the ground, but it was so muddy, I didn't.

It took the usual half-hour to set up. Even though it was early afternoon I called my nephew in Ann Arbor. No one was at home. I busied myself walking around the campground and meeting some of the recent arrivals.

Their names were Hollie and Tania Triplett from Lima, Ohio and they were pulling a fifth wheel much larger, and far more luxurious, than mine. Although they were in their middle to late fifties, they had been married only a few years, a second marriage for both. We had been walking outside in the cool air so when I was invited in for a coffee, I accepted. The coffee became a glass of wine and a glass of wine became an invitation to join them for dinner. I didn't hesitate. I loved the company. We found the Pickle Barrel Restaurant that had been recommended by the owners of the campground on one of the country roads just a few miles away. The restaurant was filled with memorabilia from the thirties, forties and fifties so everywhere we looked there was something to remark and even reminisce about. It was around five in the afternoon, there was little dinner traffic and only a few others occupying any of the seats. The service was terrific.

How long had it been since I had had a corned beef sandwich and fries? I couldn't remember. It was delicious.

We were back at the campground by six and I called Robert again. Laura, his wife, answered.

"Since it's almost dark," I said after a few brief pleasantries, "why don't I come over tomorrow."

"Come now," Laura insisted, "we haven't seen you in over a year and you've never seen the baby. We want to see you."

"I hate driving in the dark in a strange city," I reminded her.

"Auntie Joei," she said, "it's really easy to find. You have the directions."

"Yes," I confessed, "Robert sent them to me while I was still in Florida. Okay, I'll see you soon."

To make a long story short and boring, it was around six forty-five when I called from a convenience store in downtown Ann Arbor. Their answering machine picked up and I assumed that one or both were taking care of the baby. I left a long newsy message about being lost in downtown Ann Arbor and that I was going back to the campground while I was still able to find it. I would call when I got there.

Robert answered the phone. "Did you get your sense of direction from your father?" he asked knowing that Ole Fred could get lost three blocks from the house he had lived in for more than ten years and in a city that he had resided in for over fifty years.

"Do you mind." I answered rather indignantly. "Are you aware that I made it all the way to Alaska by myself," I reminded the son of my oldest brother.

"I know," he answered, "but which way were you headed?"

We both enjoyed his bit of humor and had a good laugh. I read the directions to him, told him where I had turned off the highway, and he corrected the instructions. We made a date for dinner the next day.

I spent the next morning hours looking for a storage unit large enough to accommodate the treasures that I didn't want to take with me. It would be such a relief to put heavy boxes of handmade pottery dishes, spare suitcases, an end table made of mahogany the base of it carved into an elephant, pictures and knickknacks into a safe place. After a half dozen dead-end leads I discovered that the self-storage company was walking distance from the campground. I inspected it, paid for six months and went back to the campground to transfer all the boxes into the bed of the truck. The owner/manager waited for me to return and helped remove the tailgate from the truck and put it into my storage unit. I could now attach my trailer alone. I was starting to feel a little more independent.

Dinner with Robert that Friday night consisted of burgers on the grill after we had nibbled on all the leftovers in the refrigerator. Laura worked late and I had the pleasure of meeting my great niece, Dena Ilana, for the first time. She was a tiny bit of a thing. She was cute as a button.....but incredibly tiny. That is not a word we use to describe a family member very often. Obviously she took after Laura side of the family. At eighteen months she walked and ran and talked in long sentences that astounded anyone who heard her for the first time because she was so small. She was adorable.

It was around ten when I left. Laura was not home yet. The baby was in bed. Robert was tired and I still had a half-hour drive in relatively unfamiliar territory. It had been a full and eventful day. I retraced my journey and had no trouble finding my way home.

Chapter 19

A Great Day

It was an enjoyable three-day stay. Late Saturday morning a twenty-two and a half foot fifth wheel Wanderer, pulled by a red Chevy pickup truck and driven by a slim, handsome, dark-haired man in his fifties, pulled into the campground. I think he was as surprised to see my Wanderer as I was to see his. After paying the price of admission he pulled into the site next to mine making it look like a small, intimate camping rally. This was the first time each of us had come across anyone else in this particular fifth wheel and although it was all new to me he had been on the road for months.

He was a retired FBI agent. His new career was in the private sector doing drug testing for corporations all over the eastern United States. Although his trailer was just a few months old, he had logged a couple of hundred thousand miles with it, he confided. I was delighted to see how well it had withstood the grueling road test. To date he had had no problems with it whatsoever.

He showed off the wire shelves he had built into the closets making them far more practical. That was when I learned how many features had come included in his package that had been omitted from mine and all costing him thousands of dollars less. His Wanderer was equipped with a microwave oven, television antennae, a clock and an additional battery. He too had chosen the trailer with the bunk beds because of the extra storage.

He checked over my trailer, making sure the pump worked which I had never tested. He explained a few things about what kind of battery to get and showed me where to have it installed. He suggested a few tools to keep on hand at all times like a tire pressure gauge and to invest in a compressor when I had a little extra to spend. He opened a box of flares and insisted I keep a couple of them under my seat. He handed me a sample-sized can of WD40. "You just never know when you might need these things," he said, "and keep them in your truck."

I never did find out his name. I probably would not recognize him if we met someplace away from the Wanderer but for all the gentlemen out there who take the time to help a fellow traveler, new or experienced, may I say thank you. When we parted I was feeling a notch more comfortable about my choice of trailer. His was in such good shape considering the amount of miles it had on it. It did not seem the worse for wear despite the fact that it was overloaded with drug testing supplies and pamphlets while mine was overloaded with books. Also he was traveling with two dogs to keep him company, which should have added to the disarray but it didn't. It just made it appear homey. He went to work around two and I called Robert.

I spent a part of the day enjoying a walk through the park with Robert, Laura, Dena and their friends Paul and Mary Russell. There was a path through a wooded area and another that ran around a lake. Feeling rather energetic we walked both. It was a day filled with the warmth that only good friends and family can provide and sunshine. The conversation flowed like we had been friends for years. In the tranquil setting it was hard to believe that we were in the middle of a metropolis like Ann Arbor. Paul and Mary, avid travelers, were interested in all the parts of the world that I loved. While Laura pushed Dena on the swings the conversation continued.

Over a delicious meal of barbecued steak, something I had not had in quite awhile, mushrooms, fresh bread and salad we talked long into the night.

I was back at the campground just before the gates locked at midnight.

Chapter 20

Lost

The year was 1967. I was twenty-three years old. I had left my home several weeks before in Los Angeles, California and returned to Montreal, Canada temporarily. I needed gall bladder surgery and there could be no one better than my mother to take care of me after the operation. I was released from the hospital on a Friday in August, the exact date escapes me at this moment. I changed into a pair of jeans that I zipped part way up leaving the last remaining teeth unzipped and the button undone so it would not irritate an incision that was less than a week old and still raw. I got into my 1967 dark blue Toyota Corona and drove over to my friend's house.

When I returned to the doctor's office the following Friday to have the stitches removed he advised me that I could get back to driving in about a week or so.

"Well," I answered, "you'd better find someone who'll drive me home then. I've been driving all week," I told the horrified doctor.

A week later, having been given the official okay to drive, I said goodbye to my friends and family. It was time to head back to Los Angeles since my job would not be held indefinitely. I would be leaving on Monday morning. It was on that Sunday that the Detroit riot started. Foolishly I really didn't think it would affect me.

I approached the U.S. border, was advised about the riot and asked where I was heading. "Home to Los Angeles," I responded. Had I not had American license plates on my car I would have been turned back. They gave me a safe route to follow to the highway I needed heading west. I found the entrance, sped onto the highway and as soon as I passed the next exit I realized I was heading east. I got off the highway. There was no entrance back onto the highway going west. I drove up and down some of the side streets looking for signs.

There was nothing. I found another main street. I looked up and down at each cross street hoping for anything that would indicate where to get back onto the highway. Nothing. The part of the city I was in was devoid of human life. There was no one walking. There were no cars. Businesses were closed. Some stores were boarded up. Some shops were broken open. There were fires in the distance that I could see. I was terrified.

An old battered truck with an elderly black man behind the wheel pulled up beside me at the traffic light. "Where the hell are you going lady?" he shouted.

"I'm lost. I need highway 12 going west," I said.

"Lady, stay close behind and follow," he shook his head at me shouted through the open window.

I don't know how many side streets we went up and down. I stayed as close as I dared like I could lose the only other vehicle on the road. It took just long enough for me to worry that he was leading me astray. My following stopped at the on ramp to the entrance of the highway. He motioned me to go and kept waving his hand as if telling me to go fast.

I breathed a heavy sigh of relief only after I found Interstate 75 heading south and was a long way out of Detroit.

It is a day that stands out in my mind as clearly today and it did back in 1967. That was the first time I got lost in Detroit. I have been lost in Detroit on every trip since, without fail. In recent years I have driven through that damn city twice a year always on my way to and from Florida and can never make my way through without some kind of incident.

For those of you who are now asking yourselves what's her point or has she lost her mind or better yet, has she forgotten what book she's writing, let me get back to my nephew, his family and Ann Arbor, Michigan.

Although I still had a few days to relax before driving into Canada I decided that it would be best if I did the dirty deed on a Sunday when traffic would be at a minimum and, even if there was lots of traffic, it would not be rush hour.

Robert advised me to just stay on Interstate 94 all the way to the "Bridge to Canada." There are signs everywhere and it's "impossible to get lost," he said. He understood my reasoning for wanting to leave on a Sunday.

I cleaned up quickly that morning. I had already been up for hours and as nervous as I could be. I had only one cup of coffee. My stomach was in a knot. I checked and rechecked the maps as if they would change with each viewing. By nine in the morning I was road ready. I had been on the I-94 so many times since my arrival I had no trouble finding the entrance heading east. There was little traffic.

The closer I got to Detroit the more anxious I became. The gas pedal vibrated uncontrollably. The highway was broken and cracked and potholed. At one point the back wheels of my truck hit a deep pothole, my trailer jumped and I thought the trailer had disconnected from the truck. Stupidly I pulled over to the soft shoulder of the highway, got out of the truck and slid between the truck and the trailer to make sure the fifth wheel was still attached and the metal bar still prevented its release. It all seemed okay. I got back into the truck and continued.

Horror upon horror! They were doing some construction work on the I-94 and all traffic was being diverted onto a surface street. I pulled off onto route 12 and drove directly into a gas station with lots of room to maneuver. I checked the fifth wheel hitch again. It still looked okay.

I had about nine or ten miles to drive through a derelict part of town to the "Bridge to Canada." At least one telephone pole in every block on that route, during the entire trip, had a sign on it that said "Bridge to Canada." I seemed to be following a short string of cars with Ontario license plates so I was feeling a little more secure. I was driving along slowly with the rest of the group. In the middle of the last block there was the sign that said "Bridge to Canada" with an arrow pointing straight ahead.

There were no signs at the end of that street that went either left or right. The car ahead of me, driven by an Asian man in his thirties, went straight. I followed. We are now wandering around what looked like an Industrial Park. He stopped his car and came back to talk to me.

"Where the hell did the signs to Canada go?" he asked.

"I don't know," I said suddenly feeling like the rug had been pulled out from under me and tears started welling up in my eyes, "but please don't leave me here. I will never find my way out of the downtown area," that I could now see looming large in the distance.

He stopped a short way down the road, still in the Industrial Park. He asked a woman that was out walking a dog. She used hand gestures and talked for a while always pointing straight ahead. The man in the car motioned me forward. I followed not having a clue as to where we were going.

We rounded the corner. The traffic ahead was stopped and I suddenly found myself at the entrance to the Tunnel to Canada. I paid the fee. In a voice that I know sounded strangled and squeaky said, "What the hell happened to the Bridge to Canada?"

"Don't worry," she said as she gave me change from the five dollar bill that I had given her, "you won't have a problem getting through."

I stopped at Customs. The look on my face must have told the story. "Are you going to leave the trailer in Canada?" she asked.

Chapter 21

Safe At Home

Taken aback by the question, I said, "No, why, I just bought it."

"How long will you be staying in Canada?" she asked never answering my previous question.

"The summer," I responded without hesitation.

She took a quick look inside my passport and motioned me on my way.

I breathed a little sigh of relief. The last forty miles from Ann Arbor, Michigan to Windsor, Ontario had been frightening. It was only after crossing the border that I realized the reason for the vibration in the truck. It was my trembling foot on the accelerator. The trembling stopped as soon as I hit the wide open smooth surfaced Canadian highway, which was a short drive beyond Windsor. I pulled into the first rest area with a restaurant. I went inside dragging along with me an armload of camping books. I ordered a Kentucky Fried two-piece chicken dinner and settled down to find a campground within the next fifty miles or closer if possible. It was still only late morning but I had had enough tension for one day.

I checked all the black dots on the Ontario map where the campgrounds seemed to be close to the highway in all the small towns along the way. It was too early in the season and I was out of luck. The only campground open on Sunday, April 19 was in Milton, Ontario, forty miles west of Toronto. Like it or not, I still had over two hundred miles to drive. When I left the restaurant the rain had just started.

Only in a few spots did the rain threaten to do me in. I had visions of having to stop in a deserted rest area to spend the night. But I didn't. I just kept plodding along. I stopped a couple of times for coffee making myself more and more jittery from the caffeine and thinking that I would have to drive in the dark. That thought really terrified me. It was still early afternoon but the rain made it feel late in the day. The sky was dark and ominous. I consoled myself with the fact that if I really got too nervous, if the rain started coming down heavier or if it got darker, I would pull off the road and stay in a motel.

Like the proverbial tortoise I just kept driving at a slow and steady pace. The rain finally dissipated but it did not get any lighter.

The campground I was looking for was just a few miles off the highway but when it came to concession roads I was useless. I needed to be careful. Shades of driving around the hills south of Cincinnati sprang to mind and since I had had enough driving two hundred miles back I didn't want to miss the side road. I didn't. The seven mile drive down that last country road seemed to take forever. The sign into the campground had been partially obliterated by a low hanging tree branch and if I had not been overly vigilant I certainly would have missed it.

"Please, please, please be open," I prayed in a whisper as I pulled down the last side road and onto the driveway. I stopped at the gate.

Open, by God, it was crowded. They had to check to see where they could fit me in. It didn't take them long, however, to find a small pull-thru for me, and my little camper.

I wasn't taking any chances. "I'll stay for a week." I said. "Can I pay by check?"

Still unfamiliar with all the workings and goings on with the trailer it took the usual half-hour or more to try and level the camper and to set it up. I took all the bits and pieces off the floor. I eagerly set up my television set. I plugged in my computer and printer. I made myself a well-deserved cup of tea. I went for a walk around the campground to see where all the license plates were from. Most were from Ontario. I attached the magnetic signs to the sides of my truck that indicated my name, the fact that I was an author/lecturer and had a picture of my book cover, Restless From The Start, on it.

I wanted to kiss the ground. I was home.

Chapter 22

Who Are You and Where Did You Come From

My vagabond life lasted one year and seven days. I would love to be able to conjure up an image of pulling into a perfectly manicured park with multicolored, manufactured houses situated on their own double-wide lots along side a well maintained campground for the transient population. I would describe the various motorhomes, travel trailers and fifth wheels parked side by side for the night in the middle of the a wonderful State or Province. There a handsome man would be holding his arms open to me waiting for my passionate embrace. Sorry, even my imagination does not run that wild.

My vagabond life ended on a day filled with sunshine and the promise of an easy travel day a little after ten o'clock in the morning. It ended with a bang on Interstate 65 heading north approximately twenty miles south of Louisville, Kentucky.

For the time being, however, twenty-one intimidating and nerve-wracking days into my life on the road, I was safe. For one brief moment I took a deep satisfying breath, leaned back on my bed and visualize the beach on the island of Tobago, a part of the world that Paul and I had frequented. I could see the palm trees swaying like hula dancers to the rhythm of the gentle breezes. The sand, sun-baked warm and cornstarch white, displaces as I wiggle to sink into it. I cover my bare suntanned legs with its silkiness allowing the granules to sift through my playful fingers. I lift the Pina Colada to my parched lips, sipping, allowing the coconut sweetness to linger for an instance before I swallow. Paradise.

That was the feeling that night in my trailer in Milton, Ontario. Paradise. I was home. I had unhitched and put everything in its place. I wasn't going anywhere in the near foreseeable future. It was perfect and for the first time, in what seemed like an eternity, I felt safe.

Before the week was up, still not ready to move, I paid for the balance of the month. As much as I wanted to rest and recuperate my body, mind and spirit and just plain veg, I could not stay idle. There was too much work to be done.

One morning in Toronto I saw my family doctor and had a complete physical. On another afternoon I saw my dentist taking more time than was necessary because I was one of his first patients and we always shared the events of the previous six months as he cleaned and flossed and X-rayed. My income tax had to be filed and again it took more time than necessary because my accountant was a friend of my late husband's and needed to know what I had been up to. For every appointment I drove the forty miles into Toronto taking care of whatever was necessary and visiting friends and former business associates while in the city.

It was on a Friday afternoon that I returned to the campground after my dentist visit. Although the front part of the campground was almost full when I left, the back lot had been almost totally vacant. I returned to discover that it had filled to capacity with motorhomes, trailers, fifth wheels, truck campers, a bunch of multicolored tents and a few cars that gave every impression that they were going to be home for the night for some unfortunate few.

As I walked back to find out who these people were I was grabbed, hugged, kissed by a few and congratulated by many. "Who the hell are you folks?" I asked displaying a wide grin so they would know I was friendly and really didn't mind the hugs even by strangers.

"We're an RVing Square Dance Club," volunteered a giant, gray-haired man in his sixties, his dark framed glasses sitting at half-mast. "Aren't you one of our new members?" he asked just beginning to blush at the thought of hugging a total stranger who had no idea what was going on.

"No," I replied, "I'm a guest in the park. That's my trailer there," pointing to my Wanderer parked at the end of the middle row but across the roadway that circled the main part of the campground.

Just before recognizing a few friends in the distance, "join our club," he said, "great fun and lots of exercise. Keeps this old belly at bay," he said grabbing his middle firmly with both hands.

He had just turned away when a short pudgy woman came to greet me. "Are you new to our club?" she asked.

"No," I answered again, "I'm just a guest in the park."

"You'll have to come watch us tonight," she said and immediately went into her sales pitch hoping to attract a new member. "We dance tonight in our street clothes. Tomorrow we start with a devotional, followed by a pancake breakfast and at two we have a guest speaker. Tomorrow night we dance in costume. Come join us tomorrow night as well," she said. "We always have a wonderful time."

Before walking around and meeting a bunch of the other dancers I promised I would be there to watch them that evening. As a matter of fact I looked forward to the event. I love square dancing. I love music, any and all kinds, but the livelier the better.

I walked into the hall that evening around seven. I was there even before the music had started and immediately found a seat next to one of the ladies I had met earlier in the day. It didn't take long to get back into a long conversation about camping and dancing and the guest speaker for the next day. I was suddenly filled with envy. It was going to be a lecture that I would have loved and would really have found necessary for my life on the road. He would be speaking about fixing up your camper to make it more comfortable and suiting it to your needs. I said nothing.

I sat back on my bench seat enjoying the dancing and letting my feet tap to the music and snapping my fingers that I did almost unconsciously. I was moving so much in my chair I might as well have been up there on the dance floor. I didn't miss a beat and was disappointed when eleven o'clock rolled around and the music stopped. It was time to leave. Although small groups left together I walked out alone.

There was an official club member bidding everyone a good night. It was now or never, I thought.

"I'm a brand new full time RVer," I said to the matronly woman standing at the door, "do you think anyone in your group would mind if I sat quietly at the back and listened to your guest speaker tomorrow afternoon.

"To be honest with you," she answered with a touch of annoyance in her voice "he backed out at the last minute. We have no guest speaker."

"Would you like one?" I asked.

Chapter 23

Back To Work

"Excuse me," she said, her eyebrows knitting together to form a crease in her forehead.

"I've written a book of short stories about my various trips," I volunteered, "and I lecture on world travel. I am an entertaining speaker. That's entertaining as opposed to motivational," I corrected, not wanting to appear overly boastful. "I do one lecture on Morocco. I spent three months traveling around Turkey by myself. I drove from Sarasota, Florida to Alaska by myself." I stopped talking instantly when her hand went up close to my face and she called to the Wagon Master to come over. She told him about my offer and he was instantly in agreement.

"What do you charge?" was the next question and in that one eager instant I blew a magnificent opportunity.

"All I ask is an opportunity to sell my book," I said. "I'm doing a lecture on Alaska here in the campground on Sunday so I have some flyers made up. Care to walk me back to my camper and I'll give you a couple of them," I said.

I was delighted with this new development. I had been back in Canada approximately ten days. All my chores and appointments had been taken care of, my second book Everyone's Dream Everyone's Nightmare was in the editing stage, and I had already been booked for two lectures. Given a choice of five different lectures I was only slightly surprised that both had chosen Alaska. My life was definitely heading in the right direction. I slept well that night.

I awoke to brilliant but cool sunshine. The day was perfect. I printed out a few notes. I did not intend to use them as props but I needed an opportunity to review them for the names of the places that I had visited. It had been three years since my trip to Alaska and I had taken so many trips in between it became confusing.

The group assembled a little before two and I was ready. Mr. Wagon Master introduced me by reading from the flyer I had given him the night before.

"I am a full-time, solo RVer," I said confidently looking over the group of about seventy-five, all comfortably dressed, "and easily could have taken over from the speaker that did not show up today, however, I felt I might lack credibility. I've been a full-time RVer for.....what's the date?" I said to one of the women sitting in the front row.

"May second," she replied.

"I've been a full-time RVer for thirty-one days," I said. I waited several seconds for the laughter to subside. "I now travel twelve months of every year. Until March thirtieth of this year I have been traveling for at least six months of every year."

I explained how I got stranded in Florida. I knew I had their full attention when I heard a deep sigh and a hush fell over the room. Of all my Alaska stories they loved the one about my square dancing experience. I had pulled my rig, a Volkswagen Westphalia at the time, into a campground in Palmer, Alaska. That evening they were having a square dance group meet in their auditorium and I went to watch. When they found out I had taken a lesson or two they insisted I join the dancing. It was just one of those nights when everything went wrong. They went left I went right and vice versa. The woman dancing opposite me was more than enthusiastic when the music stopped and that dance was over.

"You were wonderful," she gushed.

I was sure she was being sarcastic. "What are you talking about," I said, trying to defend myself, "when everyone went left I went right. I have no idea what I'm doing out there."

"That's your partners fault," she said. "He's not leading you properly. Girlie," she continued, "you're in Alaska now. We don't take the blame for anything. Get used to it."

The lecture and the question-and-answer period lasted over an hour. Several came up to check out my book and a few bought. A pudgy gray-haired woman in jeans and a T-shirt approached to talk.

"I'm in charge of special events for our church," said Thelma Hearn. "Would you like to do a lecture on Monday?"

"Of course," I answered, never giving it a second thought.

The rest of the day was a bit of a blur. That evening I watched as the square dancers showed up in black-and-white costumes with a few guests from another club dressed in shamrock green-and-white. Again my toes tapped and fingers popped at every change of song. Almost everyone that had been to my lecture came up to say hello and to tell me how much the entire group had enjoyed it. Many approached just to introduce themselves and apologized for missing what they heard was a terrific story. That evening I sold more books. The Wagon Master had asked that I bring a few copies since several of the dancers had mentioned that they wanted one. Before the evening was over I had been thanked by almost everyone personally and from the podium which embarrassed me no end.

The day had been such a spectacular success I was sure it would continue into the next. How could it not, I wondered. I had done so much promoting around the campground with door to door flyers and several put up in the washrooms and office. Many of the campers had expressed an interest in coming to hear about Alaska. I was very disappointed when only five people showed up. One of the attendees was the husband of the campground owner, an Alzheimer patient. It was an extremely difficult presentation. I did the best I could.

Monday started with another lecture at the Boston Presbyterian in Halton Hills. Since there was no preparation I did bits and pieces of several lectures.....one that I call Solo World Travel encompassing a summer of archaeological digging in England, three months touring Turkey and a bit of my Alaska adventure. Within an hour I was off to visit fellow camping friends, Richard and Beverley Hood in Whitby, Ontario, a seventy-five mile drive.

Chapter 24

Drip! Drip! Drip!

Richard and Beverley Hood started as camping friends and were quickly elevated to people I love having in my life. Richard towers over me, a rare treat since I am of formidable height and weight myself. His dark hair is in sharp contrast to tall and statuesque Beverley's, premature, pure white and always neatly coiffed. Both seem to share an open-heart policy.

In 1995 recently having purchased a Volkswagen Westphalia motorhome for my solo trek to Alaska, Richard and Beverley had been president and secretary of the Westphalia club. I had been fortunate enough to have them both at the same camping rally when I was learning all the ins and outs of its operation. Along with all the other special equipment that my VW had was something called an 'easy-to-assemble add-on room.' When it took everyone at the Westphalia Rally several hours to figure out how to attach the tent and get it sorted, assembled and up, I decided that it was never going to be used. It was only one of the many extras I left stored in the Hood's garage.

My fully loaded, to the point where I needed two hands to lift it, toolbox was another item left behind. "If it takes that many tools to fix it you'll need a mechanic anyway," was Richard's advice. I took the few tools that he recommended for minor jobs that I would and could do myself. The rest, housed in a heavy blue metal chest, remained in his garage along with four spare tires without rims, a giant, puke-green waste water tote and other bits and pieces that came with the van. Some of these bits and pieces we could not figure out what they were for or where they belonged.

Now that I was a solo, full-time road warrior we had even more to talk about. We did much of the talking over a delicious, home cooked and in a real home (without wheels, fancy that) spaghetti dinner. Their son Christopher joined us for dinner only but did little to contribute to the conversation. We were never far from talking of our trips, many of which we had discussed before but still enjoyed reminiscing about. By the time the evening was over my throat felt scratchy. A week of hell followed.

If I had had a phone on one of those middle of the nights I might have been tempted to call 911 or a girlfriend living forty miles away in Toronto, however, I was not so equipped. I lay there unable to stop or control deep, gut wrenching coughs. The coughing went into gagging and choking. My head continued pounding long after the coughing spasm temporarily abated. I could go on to describe the stomach problems it produced but even I don't want to think about it. It turned out to be a rather violent bout of a flu strain that was going around that summer and my immune system with all its recent stresses and strains was not capable of fighting it off. I emerged from my camper two days later looking like I had just barely scared off the grim reaper. Sickly pale and gaunt looking, I went out for a short walk.

"Oh my God" remarked Tricia Kirkwood-Irvine as I wandered past her fifth wheel "you look so pale." We talked awhile.

Gil Wallace who was out wandering the campground with Lakota, a totally unmanageable and too big to be called a puppy even though he was, Rottweiler, and I walked together for a bit. He too mentioned my complexion and again I went into a short but dramatic explanation

For the rest of the week, if either did not see me on any particular day or my door was closed when it should have been open, someone knocked. Usually I was on the computer and a babbled explanation followed. I always thanked them for their concern and stopped whatever I was doing for a quick chat before returning to work.

Drip! drip! drip!

What was the noise that shattered the quiet, I wondered? My ears pricked up at this new, unexpected sound.

95

I checked the kitchen and bathroom sinks. I checked the faucet in the shower and tub. Nothing. Must be my imagination, I thought. I went back to work and lost myself for an hour or more in editing.

Drip! drip! drip!

I checked the outside connection into my trailer. No leaks. I checked the floor in the bathroom. That was dry. I checked the pipe under the bathroom sink. Nothing there. I checked the pipes under the kitchen sink. Nothing.

My ears must be bothering me from the flu, I thought. I went back to work since as soon as I moved about and made the slightest amount of noise the sound disappeared.

Drip! drip! drip!

I checked all the cabinets at floor level. I opened the door to the cubbyhole under the refrigerator and removed one soggy black Reebok walking shoe and a roll of paper towels that had kept my trailer from floating away in what surely would have been a tsunami.

"Oh, hell, what now?" I said out loud.

My discovery was made after seven in the evening. There was no one to call and I would not have known whom to call anyway. I removed a bath towel from my neat stack, soaked up the excess and felt the linoleum that had curled up on the edges. I took a pot out from the cupboard under the kitchen sink and stuck it under the drip, drip, drip. It now sounded like the beat of a drum but it was certainly not music to my ears. I put my computer to bed and sulked as I prepared an omelet for dinner.

"What a pain in the ass this trailer is turning into," I said out loud wishing there were someone with me to share the problems. Before going to bed, sprawled on my back on the floor, I stuck my hand into the narrow space between the refrigerator and the bathroom wall. Two fingers felt the drip coming from the shower hose and it quickly ran down my forearm. The bolt was too high up and I could not reach it to grip or tighten it. I emptied the cup or so of water that had collected in the bottom of the pot.

I fell asleep listening to drip, drip, drip.

I awoke listening to drip, drip, drip and emptied half a pot of water. It was too early to call anyone. I was on the phone with the dealer in Florida just as they switched on the lights to start their day. I wanted my problem to be their problem. The salesman that I had dealt with when I purchased the trailer transferred me to their service department who guaranteed they would pay for all the repairs that had to be made.

The campground office in Milton Heights recommended a company called Under The Stars in Mississauga, Ontario who did warranty work and would come out to the campground. Rene took my call. We set up an appointment for the last call of his day and all he could do was guarantee that he would get there that day and "yes, he would do the work under warranty."

He arrived just as the sun was going down around eight in the evening. He left around nine-thirty. I listened for the drip, drip, drip. There was only silence as I fell asleep.

Chapter 25

Country Living

Temporarily I had had enough and desperately wanted and needed a change. Almost every evening, after my nightly walk, I returned to discover something grotesque had invaded my twenty-two and a half feet of space. One night it was a spider, the size of which didn't matter since any and all of them caused hyperventilation to my delicate system. On another occasion it was something big, brown, disgusting and flying that left a splat on the wall when I smacked it with a rolled up magazine. One evening I saw something so large I thought it was a bumble bee in the corner of the room near the head of my bed. It turned out to be a giant black ant. I actually heard the crunch when I caught it in a wad of paper towels. Oh, yuk!

Trailer life wasn't all it was cracked up to be. I was very intimidated pulling it, always wondering if a tire had gone flat and was chewing up the undercarriage of my home or, heaven forbid, had fallen off entirely. I worried constantly about getting lost in unfamiliar territory, like the back roads south of Cincinnati, and not being able to back it up or turn around. I worried about some jackass cutting me off on the highway and not being able to stop in time. To make matters worse most of my fears had already happened to some degree.

The living space was small and I hadn't as yet found space to display my few remaining treasures and the clutter depressed me. Crawling around on my hands and knees during the recent flu epidemic had not been fun and, quite frankly, scared the hell out of me. Still, I had planned on pulling it to Montreal to visit my friends and family and then pulling it back to Toronto to do the same. When my Montreal friends, Joan and Cary Dressler insisted I stay with them as I had always done in the past, the decision was made for me.

"You can park your trailer in our driveway," said Joan, "but you'll sleep in YOUR bedroom."

I knew also that a bed awaited me at Arlene Kravitz's apartment in Toronto on my return trip.

Arlene and Joan, although not friends to each other, have been dear to me since our high school days. While they have both lived active but stationary lives I have lived a somewhat transient existence for most of my adulthood. My friends were used to my popping in and out of their lives. Well to be brutally honest I have been a constant in their lives. I just pop in and out of their homes every now and then. Gratefully, I have always been made to feel welcome and since they never know from which direction I have hailed, a lively conversation usually ensues. So sure am I of their open door policy where I am concerned that I once called Joan from a store a mile away and when she asked when I would be arriving I suggested she put the phone down slowly and open the front door. For those who know me well and best said with a British accent, the expression Cheeky Devil comes to mind.

I had been in the Milton Heights campground for one month to the day. I was well rested and recuperated. I cleaned out the refrigerator giving the few perishables to my neighbor. I packed my well used-and-abused blue canvas bag making sure my computer and printer, paper, envelopes and extra disks were well cushioned. Clothing always seemed to be incidental in my life and especially so now that I was living in limited space. I enjoyed working in the middle of most nights and doing the bulk of my editing work wearing nothing but an old T-shirt and comfy sweat pants with very little stretch left in the waistband. It didn't take long to pack even though I had to dig out a few niceties from their hiding places. I couldn't let everyone see me in my ratty-tatty work clothes.

I hitched up the trailer, hauled it around like an old pro before delivering it to the far end of the campground. It was to be put amongst the many others that awaited their owners. Under the guidance of a very competent staff member I backed it into a spot where the grass had not grown too high and had a bit of gravel rather than just dirt under the wheels. It would be easily accessible when I returned.

I leveled it, checked to make sure the innards were secure and finally detached it from the truck. I walked around the outside of the trailer for one last inspection, making sure all the windows were closed, the door double locked and the roof vents down. I hopped back into the truck feeling a little freer and drove up to the office. I paid for a month of storage and said goodbye to some of the staff and the owner.

I breathed a sigh of relief when the security gate lifted and I drove out onto the concession road. It was a short distance to the highway. I would not be traveling far this first day. Richard and Beverley Hood from Whitby awaited my arrival.

We could not have been lazier that day. Our conversation always started, ended and was interspersed with travel. Only tidbits of family life, work, bingo and other incidentals were ever mentioned and even then only in passing. Although they still maintained their beautifully landscaped and charmingly decorated two-story brick home and Richard still worked full time, they always seemed to be going or coming back from somewhere. Newfoundland, ancestral home to Beverley, had never really been in my plans until we looked at all the pictures and I heard for the umpteenth about the warmth and hospitality of the people. How could I not want to visit places called Come By Chance, Conception Bay or Heart's Content. I would have to discover for myself some day what other treasures awaited a province foreign even to other Canadians.

Dinner that evening was cooked on the barbecue, something I rarely had and loved when I did. Since I wasn't driving anywhere I sipped at a couple of glasses of Apelia Red, a taste I acquired in Greece. Their national drink, retsina, was not palatable to my taste but I loved their wine. The drip of the grape I had chosen went well with our feast as did everything else that night.

My time with the Hood's ended too soon. By ten fifteen the next morning I was on the road again. Even though I was several miles east of Toronto it was a long, boring drive, devoid of interesting sights on a straight road, mostly wooded on both sides. The billboards so prevalent on American highways are not permitted on Canadian highways. The scenery improved only slightly as I approached major cities like Kingston but it was spotty. I could, of course, have turned off the highway and taken the old highway 20 but that would have added an hour or more to an already tedious trip. Sightseeing from a vehicle, alone, has never suited me. I stopped for coffee, lunch, gas and a few pit stops. I backed onto the Dressler driveway at around four that afternoon.

"Would you really have liked another twenty feet on the back of this thing parked in your driveway," I said.

"Holy cow look at the size of it," they both kept repeating as they walked around my truck that took up most of their driveway.

"I call it my SSM," I said. "Stands for Super Stud Magnet."

"Wow, what a monster. So loud. Do you like it?" Cary asked.

"I'm really not used to the size of it yet, but, yes, I love it," I said. "I feel safe in it." "Needs eight lanes to turn around though," I offered.

It was a quiet evening that followed. We talked. I called my brothers and my nieces, a local call for the first time in months, making arrangements to see them all at various times over the next few days. I went to bed early that night since that trip always wore me down. I awoke in the middle of the night. I red light glowed eerily above my head.

"Oh my God, where the hell am I," suddenly feeling panicked, my heart thumping in my chest. I waited daring not to move or breathe. Slowly my eyes adjusted to the darkness. In a few seconds I recognized the window covered by familiar sheer curtains and the mirrored dresser outlined in the shadows. I reached over and turned on the lamp. My breathing returned to normal. The feeling of doom slowly evaporated when I realized the bloodshot "eye" must be part of their security or fire alarm systems. Sleep eluded me the rest of the night and I wished I were back in my camper and could make myself a cup of coffee and play computer games.

I stayed a few days to catch up on each other's lives. I mowed their lawn, front and back, one afternoon and enjoyed the exercise. We went out for a steak dinner to a favorite inn not far, in country miles, from their home. Joan and I drove to my post office box in Hawkesbury, Ontario to retrieve my mail. The three of us walked to a campground near their home and I checked out the license plates and discovered that most were from Quebec. We stopped for a dish of homemade ice cream on the way back. It didn't take me long to become agitated with all the tranquillity. Country living was not for me. I needed lots of people around.....strangers mostly telling of exciting experiences, new places that I must see and different people they had met. I needed shop windows to look into as I wandered aimlessly. I needed to be able to walk on pavement to a McDonald's for a McFlurry.

I moved into town.

Chapter 26

The Reunion

Life with Harry was always a series of adventures and misadventures. Although he and his significant other, Sandra, were always heading off someplace, they frequently did it in different directions. Sandra loves shopping, window and otherwise, and Harry is mildly addicted to exercise. They both work so I was alone much of the time.

I did, however, join Harry at the YMHA for Friday noon exercise classes led by a dark-haired, skinny guy in black silky shorts and T-shirt, standing on a platform and speaking through a microphone attached to a headset. I followed the group trying to keep up with people who did this every day. My hours at the "Y" also gave me an opportunity to see my older brother Nathan, also addicted to exercise, for the first time.

In between warm up, cool down and calisthenics, with or without various sizes of barbells, the routine included walking at a steady clip around the gym. I quickly fell into line with another lady, about my age. She too was walking alone. We talked as we walked neither one of us looking familiar to the other until we mentioned our maiden names and the school we had attended. Both of us had spent a torturous amount of time at Baron Byng High School. Although prestigious in its day it had long since closed its doors.

As we dressed, Hilda, my tall, well-shaped walking partner mentioned that some relatives were coming in from California that afternoon so she had to hurry off.

"Are your relatives formerly from Montreal?" I asked just to keep the conversation open.

"Yes, they moved to Los Angeles in the sixties," she answered. "My aunt Doris died in August. My Uncle Moe and cousins Sandi and Terry are coming in."

"Moe Rubin is your uncle?" I asked, never dreaming I would recognize the entire family by their first names alone.

"You know them?" her eyes widened as they met mine.

"Moe and Doris were best friends with my parents. Sandi I remember was a snob. But we were both about fifteen at the time, what did we know. I don't believe this," I said.

"I'm having Sunday brunch. Please come," invited Hilda. "My brother will be there also. He too went to Baron Byng."

"I wouldn't miss it for the world," I answered as I wrote out her telephone number and would call her for an address and directions as the day neared.

I changed quickly and waited for Harry to shower and change. One of the reasons I enjoyed Fridays at the "Y" was the extracurricular activity afterwards.....lunch. Harry would meet a bunch of his jogging cronies at a Vietnamese Restaurant for one of the most incredible soups I had ever tasted complete with bok choy, sliced pork and long dangling noodles. My mouth was watering long before we reached the restaurant.

As we drove the few blocks I told Harry about my invitation to Sunday Brunch. Harry too remembered the family and was saddened to hear about Doris. "I don't remember what she looked like," said Harry, "but I always remembered the cigarette dangling from her lips. Emphysema, what a killer," he said, not having to remind me that our father had suffered the same fate.

Lunch with the entourage had been something I looked forward to. I sat at the table with six men and only one of them was related. How unlike Florida, I reminisced silently, where eight women overwhelmed every guy. I reveled in the uniqueness of the situation and listened to talk of investments, the next marathon, a few problems with their adult children coming home.....just for a short while to get their act together was the usual excuse, and what sixty-three year old stud was dating what thirty year old bombshell. The conversation was the same in every country and in every language, I presume, and it soon bored me. It didn't take me long to become disinterested especially after the soup was gone. I was not unhappy when lunch was over and we went back home for a few computer games that Harry and I played on his television set. The days passed.

I arrived at Hilda's home late morning and when it took several minutes to answer the door I worried that I either had the wrong house, the wrong day or had arrived much too early. None of the above was the case. I think it was a question that each thought the other had answered the door and no one moved until it rang for the third time.

Moe, in his eighties, was a fine looking man. He stood straight and tall with just the hint of a paunch, so prevalent in men over twenty-five. His hair still had a few dark strands interspersed with the gray and a smile so warm and friendly I could not resist a hug. I would have recognized him anywhere. Salt and pepper gray and far (very far) from bean-pole thin, he surely would have passed me on the street. Knowing that I was Fred and Zelda's daughter, however, made all the difference in the world.

"I'm so sorry to hear about Doris," I said as he hugged me closer.

I was introduced to daughter Terry. If I had met her while they lived in Montreal she would have been much too young for me to care about.

Sandi too had changed from that tall, skinny kid. She was no longer 'stuck up' as we used to like to call it. Like her father her posture was elegant. The shorts and matching blouse outfit she wore came from the boutiques of Northern California and fit the mature woman standing in front of me. Her blond hair, recently coiffed in the latest style, gave her that easy-going Californian look. Only the sadness in her pretty face belied the situation. Two weeks before the death of her mother, who had asked to be taken off a feeding tube, her young husband, Mike, had died of heart failure.

I listened, tears stinging my eyes. It was a conversation so filled with sadness that it could not sustain itself.

When Hilda's brother Arthur arrived, it was another face that did not look the least bit familiar even though we had gone to high school together. He was a year or two older than Hilda and me. When I looked at our year book I recognized him instantly. In person.....bearded, balding and wearing glasses.....not a chance.

The brunch lasted from noon to after three in the afternoon. Different conversations were going on in different parts of the kitchen and in different rooms. The table was filled with traditional Jewish foods that I had not tasted in years. Plates were loaded with fresh bagels. There was lox and cream cheese. One platter had delicious gefilte fish (finely chopped codfish and spices). I passed on that one, not liking its taste even as a child. There was a container of herring marinated in brine with onions that was out of this world. One container was filled to the brim with chopped eggplant, another delicacy from my years gone by when my mother used to prepare it. Sliced tomatoes, cucumber chunks, lettuce, sour black olives, capers, and a bowl of fruit weighed down the table as well. No Jewish meal would be complete without a braided, sliced egg bread called Challah.

We talked and we ate. I would love to be able to say that I helped clean up at the end but that had been already been done. We, and I'm including the entire group, not the royal we, had eaten almost every bit of food on the table. After all was said and done the paper plates and plastic cups were thrown into the garbage. The cutlery and the serving platters went into the dishwasher and we removed ourselves from the huge, eat-in kitchen. We plopped down on the living room sofas and chairs vowing not to eat another morsel that day.

At four o'clock we went for a walk in downtown Montreal and by six o'clock we found ourselves lined up for smoked meat sandwiches. When the line up at Schwartz's, an old Montreal tradition, was too long and cigarette smoke would have invaded every breath we took, we walked across St. Lawrence Boulevard for dinner at The Main. Our vow of "not eating another morsel that day" lasted two hours.

It was around ten-thirty in the evening that we said good night. The reunion was the highlight on my Montreal trip.

I didn't drive far when I left Montreal.

Chapter 27

A Day in the Country

My name would have been mud if I didn't stop this time. I had promised on so many other occasions that this would have been the final insult. My destination was less than a hundred miles down the road on the way back to Toronto and just a few miles off the Trans Canada Highway in the hamlet of Alexandria. It was a short commuter train ride from downtown Montreal that John and Esther Plaskon made their home, their summer home anyway.

Although John, a Montreal investment dealer, had been well acquainted with my late husband, I had met him only a few times. It was by sheer happenstance that they were back in my life.

It actually restarted in Sarasota. I was waiting for a friend outside a movie theater and a familiar looking man stood nonchalantly, leaning against the wall, at the back entrance to the Gulf Gate Mall on Stickney Point Road. He was comfortably attired in a multicolored short sleeved shirt and beige trousers. He seemed like every other tourist in Florida but much too young looking to be retired so I assumed he was just visiting. The longer I waited and watched the more familiar he looked and the more curious I became. If he glanced my way he showed no signs of recognizing me.

I still had a few minutes to wait for my friend so I approached him. "Excuse me, are you from Canada?" I asked.

"Yes," he replied, "I'm from Montreal."

"What's your name?" I questioned.

"Plaskon," he answered.

"Your first name is......," I asked, knowing his last name was the one I was hoping for.

"John," he answered.

"John," I said, "I'm Joei Hossack, Paul's wife."

108

"Oh, my God," he said, as he hugged me and called to his wife whom I had met a few less times than I had met him. "Esther look whose here. You remember Joei Hossack?"

Just as my friend Joan Papa arrived John and I were exchanging telephone numbers. Over the next few years we got together often in Sarasota since they frequented their condo on Siesta Key. I always promised, however, that I would not drive by their Canadian door without stopping.

The directions I got from Esther while still in Montreal were very precise with street names and route numbers when available and mileage when not available. Although I was not used to country distances with odd shaped trees and giant boulders as landmarks, I found it. When she heard my loud diesel truck chugging up their long winding driveway she came out to greet me.

I had forgotten how charming a country setting could be with its acres of plowed land, huge market gardens in neat rows with wispy greens just showing through and trees dwarfed by the vastness of the land. The outside of their two story brick home had been maintained to reflect the unchanging countryside. The inside had been remodeled from the oak front door with the stained glass insert to the back door that led out into the "back forty" and from the sanded, refinished and varnished floor to the new roof that covered the second story, keeping only those walls that suited them. It remained, however, a solid country home.

The tour was brief. The kitchen was unlike any other country kitchen I had ever been in and having spent a few years, fifty miles north of Toronto on some concession road south of Beeton, Ontario and before that was the proud owner of eight acres of apple, pear, and plum orchard with house, barn, milk house and numerous other out buildings in Franklin Center, Quebec, I had seen my share of country homes. This country kitchen was utilitarian only. It was not for socializing. The large wooden cupboards held colorful dishes, food stuffs and pots and pans. The ceramic bowls on the sparkling clean counters contained fruits, nuts and a few vegetables. Braided garlic bulbs from their garden hung from the hooks in the ceiling. The window looked out at the front of the house and down onto the road. Out of place were the dozens of jam jars waiting for the next batch of Esther's exquisite grape jam.

The only room off the kitchen was the dining room. A large wooden china cabinet and a hutch were the only other pieces of furniture. The massive mahogany table with padded wooden bench seats took up most of the space. We adjourned to the living room. In that room remained the only visible evidence of what the walls had been like before the renovations. In one corner the old fashioned brick wall had not been covered over and added uniqueness to a fashionable room with a comfortable two-seater couch, overstuffed lounge chairs and a large round coffee table. We made small talk before heading out for lunch. Esther was temporarily without means of transportation. Her red pickup truck was in the shop. We took mine.

The restaurant on the main street of Alexandria was a two-story affair. We entered on the street level and went downstairs for a seat with a view of the old mill still in operation. While the mill lazily scooped up the water and deposited it, a muskrat was busy foraging. I'm sure it was a muskrat. I hope it was a muskrat.

The picture window, once again, overlooked an idyllic countryside. It was early afternoon and there were few patrons in the restaurant so we could relax, enjoy our homemade burger and catch up on recent events even though we had seen each other in Sarasota only a few weeks earlier. The restaurant would be crowded for dinner, I was told.....as crowded as anything gets in Alexandria, Esther volunteered. Before returning home we picked up a few groceries.

When John returned from work he took special pride in showing me around his garden. "This," he said pointing to what would eventually be rows of carrots, onions, garlic, peppers, radishes and numerous other vegetables that I took special pride in plucking off the shelf from any one of a number of large grocery stores, "is my real source of relaxation," John confided. "I love it out here."

110

That night I slept in one of the most comfortable beds I have ever had the pleasure to test. The second story of the house contained four bedrooms that had been remodeled into three.

By mid morning I had had my fill of quiet country living and was ready to get back on the road and civilization. Once again it was a long, tedious drive to Toronto made longer by the fact that I had to stop at Arlene's office to pick up her keys. I also had to shop for a few groceries before heading back to her apartment. The minute I got my luggage, complete with computer and printer into the safety of her apartment, the heavens opened up. I was glad to be off the road.

It was two weeks of nonstop activity in Toronto. Included was lunch with my friend Anna McKendrick at a little outdoor cafe on the Danforth and coffee and pastry at a bookstore on the corner of Wolfrey Avenue. When I needed a new batch of checks from my downtown bank I decided to do it on a Friday so I could meet my accountant, Phil Layton, for lunch along with all the cronies my husband used to meet every Friday at the Strathmore Hotel. I had brunch with Maria Venczel at Movenpick Restaurant. I met with Joe Cirilla and the artist who would be designing the cover of my book Everyone's Dream Everyone's Nightmare and had dinner with Dorothy Till, a friend from.....well let's not go back there......a friend forever and no stop in Toronto would ever be complete without dinner at the McCreery's. I stopped into Chapter's, the largest bookstore chain in Canada and picked up information on getting my book into their stores. I spent an evening with Elaine Jamieson and her investment group. One day was spent on Toronto Island visiting Margaret Drew, my Toronto/Sarasota/Toronto friend. It should have been half a day but I took the wrong boat and ended up having to walk all the way around the Island. What a pain in the ass that was but a lovely day when I finally got to where I was going.

My two weeks in Toronto went by all too quickly but in the end I was anxious to get back on my own and back to work a little more steadily on my book. I returned to Milton Heights campground. What a disappointment that was. The place was empty.

Chapter 28

Niagara Falls

I paid for three days worth of camping. I retrieved the trailer from the back lot not bothering to plug in the brakes and pulled it back to its original spot and unhitched. I plugged in the electricity, attached the sewer and water hoses and checked my food stuffs making a list of groceries that I would be needing for the next few days. Grocery shopping had become a major event. I needed to get a life and an out of the way campground with few campers wasn't the one I wanted.

I drove to Niagara Falls early the next morning. It was only about sixty miles away but on a highway that had been outdated almost from the day it opened. The Queen Elizabeth Highway, better known as the QEW, was three lanes most of the time with one lane closed for construction. It stretched to four lanes at times when the road was splitting to go elsewhere and down to two lanes in other spots. At those spots traffic almost always came to a dead stop. The road was hellish with giant potholes, pieces of old tire treads strewn around and on-ramps that came right into traffic rather than slowly merging from their own lane. The highway lacked a soft shoulder for miles at a time. Traffic, put simply, was a nightmare and that was during off-hours.

Nearing the end of my journey just as the road split with one going to Fort Erie and the other going God-knows-where, I saw the sign off in the distance to Lundy's Lane. It was the main street in town and the only street in Niagara Falls that I knew. I realized in that split second that I had taken the wrong fork in the road. I got off the highway at the next exit, saw a Tim Horton's Donut Shop and decided that I needed a muffin more than I needed Lundy's Lane. Their coffee too is addictive. By the time I was through with my coffee and chocolate chip muffin I had directions to Lundy's Lane. I was to make a right turn at the next corner and drive

113

down to the bottom of the hill. I had gone out of my way about a quarter of a mile.

I turned right at the bottom of the hill and within a mile came across three campgrounds in a row. The first was a KOA. I entered the office/store to find a reasonably well stocked mini market that was jammed with kids in bathing suits. Fortunately they offered nothing in the way of discounts even if I stayed a month or two. The hordes of little kids had already turned me off. Even though I had to give up all hope of finding another campground with a hot tub I was happy to be on my way. I tried the second campground, Scott's Trailer Park, and although the monthly rate and their two-month rate was a bit expensive they had an extra special price for three months. I whipped out my checkbook and paid them for three months.

After paying the fee I walked around the campground. School was not out yet so it wasn't as busy as I knew it would be at the end of June. I watched, with a bunch of others, as a trailer was being backed into the spot where it would stay for the season or possibly forever. It was large and new. The proud owners were watching along with me but went off to inspect the inside while a small group of us lingered on the outside.

After introducing myself to a Hazel and Bill Pegg, I told them I would be checking into the campground in a couple of days and had this tiny spot to back my trailer into. "I'm not good at backing up," I told Bill, "and between trees no less."

"I'll back it in for you," he offered.

"Bill was a truck driver," Hazel volunteered, "he'll do it for you. He doesn't mind."

I thanked them both and when the trailer was centered and unhitched in its spot and several men started putting concrete blocks under it I left to continue my wandering. At the far end of the park a very pretty, heavy-set woman came over to introduce herself. "I'm Glenda Torres," she said, "we're here for the summer."

114

"I'm Joei Hossack and I'll be back in a couple of days. I'm staying for the summer. I'm writing a book and I need a quiet place to work."

"My husband, Hector, is the coach for the third string Blue Jays baseball team," she explained. "You can come to the games with me," she offered.

"That sounds wonderful. I'd love to," I gushed.

By the time I had left the campground I was thrilled with the day's events. It was just what I needed.....a busy place to recuperate and write and edit and swim and hopefully get involved in all that went on in the tourist region. There would be new campers coming and going all the time since Niagara Falls is one of the busiest tourist traffic areas in Canada and thankfully I had already made several friends.

I drove back to Milton Heights. I had one day to say goodbye to the few campers that were left. Even those few remaining would be leaving around the same time that I did. One couple, Gil and Del Wallace would be heading out east to the Maritime Provinces. Doug and Tricia Irvine would be heading north to cottage country. Author/lecturer Peggi McDonald and her husband John would be heading out west. They were hoping to lead a group of RVers to the Northwest Territories. I would be heading to Niagara Falls. It was all working itself out nicely.

I didn't sleep well the night before I left. That ole intimidation was back but I couldn't let it stop me. I cleaned up, undid the hoses and unplugged the electricity. I set all the breakables, my television set and the large wine bottle, on the floor surrounded by all the pillows. Crates that would normally be stacked I set side by side so they wouldn't fall over during the bumpy ride. It was still early when I drove out the gates and made my way back to highway 25 and headed south to the QEW. It had been over two months since I pulled the trailer on the road. My heart was pounding, my mouth was dry and my head hurt. My fingers curled to a death grip on the steering wheel. I was so nervous I was

115

about to pull over to the curb and give myself a chance to breathe.

"God," I said out loud, "I can't do this alone."

I really cannot explain what happened next. I took a deep breath, my first since I had left the campground. My heart stopped pounding. I suddenly realized that the music was on and I could hear it. Slowly I started humming along. My fingers relaxed slightly on the steering wheel. I turned onto the service road of the QEW and watched as a tractor trailer went past. The van behind the huge truck slowed, motioned me in and I was on the highway gliding smoothly into the steady flow of traffic.

I was glad that I had taken the trip a few days earlier because there were times when I had to pull into the second lane so as not to be on an off ramp exit and I knew where they were. I pulled over with time to spare. I also knew not to take the Fort Erie road and got off at Lundy's Lane without having to turn on and off side streets.

I pulled into Scott's Trailer Park, drove down my aisle, parked my truck in the middle of the road and went looking for that truck driver who promised to back in my trailer. He wasn't hard to find.

Chapter 29

Settling Down

Bliss. That is the only way to describe the feeling. I was sitting in my own camper, on my own lot, on a glorious day filled with sunshine and green grass with my computer, printer, television set, a swimming pool within a one minute walk and knowing that I wasn't going anywhere for at least three months.

It was a place to relax. It was a place to meet new people and watch the comings and goings of strangers living close enough to hear a sneeze. It was a place to regenerate, rejuvenate and work.

Walking up and down each row of my new neighborhood until the one point two mile distance was covered became a morning exercise ritual. There were always new people to meet most of whom enjoyed just sitting on a lawn chair and chatting. There was usually a new friendly four-legged creature to pet and a faraway license plate to check out. There was always something interesting to take a picture of. One photo showed a teen-aged girl who had slept on the hood of her car, her tresses covering the windshield. Another was of a giant Rottweiler that was letting a kitten get the better of him by laying across his head and batting a paw at the twitching ear. There was always something new to learn about where to visit and what to see next.

I picked up The Review, a local newspaper and discovered that the region had an active Canadian Author's Association and they were requesting "interested writers to join them in a meeting." Within a day or two of unhitching my trailer I was off to what I hoped would be an educational and entertaining session. Although the first meeting I attended was choosing new board members for their group and not really what I had in mind for a stimulating meeting, I enjoyed being back into the writing game with like-minded people. I was also invited to their annual summer picnic on the fourteenth of July at the Niagara-On-The-Lake home of the club president. Before I could get down to work properly I knew I needed cohorts. I attended their meetings regularly, made friends and worked.

Since I am in the habit of rising very early I attended several business breakfasts hoping to learn about opportunities to lecture. I tried to find a couple of Toastmasters groups and discovered that they disbanded for the summer. I picked up a Special Events calendar for the Niagara region and learned through my many phone calls that only the Rotary Club held meetings throughout the year. The Lions, Lioness, Pilot's, Kiwanis, and University clubs all took a summer hiatus and resumed the week after Labor Day. I called a local chapter of the Rotary Club and offered a free lecture. After reviewing my book Restless From The Start the date was set for July sixteenth. It was a beginning.

Much to my delight I found a singles' group, Single Professional Association of Niagara (SPAN for short) with about two hundred and fifty regularly attending members. The only nights I stayed home, after joining the club, were those that I wanted to stay home. There were weekly dinners to attend with one rather formal dinner per month plus several impromptu ones. We went to movies. We played pool. We had barbecues. We went dancing. Friday was karaoke night at a local dance joint. We went bowling, something I had not done for twenty or more years, and into my life came two women friends, both recent divorcees.

Blond, fair skinned, very attractive and athletically-built Jan Ditsch and prematurely white-haired, gently loving and soft spoken Elinor Wegener and I became a close knit threesome. Where we all went we always managed to have a good time even if we were the only ones we spoke to. Where any of us went with the other two hundred and forty-six or any part thereof something was missing. Both women are school teachers and their summers were their own. I loved the camaraderie. Before the summer was over Marina, Elinor's sister-in-law and also recently divorced, was welcomed into our exclusive little group.

In between all that was going on I stayed focused on my writing. I had a second meeting with the graphic designer in Mississauga, Ontario, for the cover of my soon-to-be-finished tome. A few of the campers read excerpts or chapters of my latest. Some gave in depth opinions, most didn't. Everyone seemed to like it. That didn't matter. The work was getting done.

On the sixteenth of July, so nervous about my lecture for the Rotary Club, I was awake around four-thirty in the morning. I had coffee, dressed and was out the door while it was still dark. I left at six not having exact directions to the hotel. It took me fifteen minutes from door to door so I had an hour or so to kill. Fortunately the morning edition of the newspaper had already been delivered and I had been given a copy by the hotel desk clerk. I sat and read, rehearsed the start of my lecture and walked outdoors for a mile high view of Niagara Falls. I had never seen the Falls from that height and they were gorgeous. The buffet-style breakfast with the usual bill of fare was delicious. My lecture on Solo World Travel was a success.

By the following Monday I had been invited to lecture at a banquet in St. Catharines, Ontario by a guest in the audience. I was contacted by the Rotary Club president and told I had been the topic of conversation at their barbecue that weekend. If they could arrange a brunch to include spouses would I be willing to do another lecture and another member of the group belonged to the International Pilot's Club and would I be interested in doing a lecture for their service group.

"Yes, yes and yes," was my answer to them all. By the end of the summer, I had been booked for sixteen lectures between September 4 and October 13. Included in that group of lectures was one to the Canadian Author's Association, the subject being Self-Publishing and Promotion.

There was time enough in between, however, to get bored. It was the tiniest ad, given to me on a rudimentary map at the campground office that caught my attention. I called the telephone number listed to see if I could pick up information to do a self-guided tour of the Freedom Trail via the Underground Railroad. The tour began in Fort Erie, Ontario, about twenty miles away from where I was staying, and ended in Niagara-On-The-Lake, a few short miles east of Niagara Falls. Even in stages and without much effort I could see it all.

In the corner of the ad were the initials B.M.E. and I couldn't resist asking Norma Tull what they stood for since the invitation for the lecture I would be doing at the banquet in September, had those initials as well.

"British Methodist Episcopal," she answered. "You're our guest speaker," she said, sounding rather excited. "I'm leaving the office in a few minutes. Why don't I bring you the packet of information. Where are you staying?" she asked.

"I'm picking up a group from the hotel almost right across the street from your campground," she replied, when I told her where I was camping. "I'll be there in about fifteen minutes."

"I'll wait for you at the office," I answered.

Instead of a handshake or a simple hello we hugged. It just seemed so natural. Her hair was red, pinned back and cropped short. Her figure was that of a mature woman, her skin was smooth and dark and her soft-spoken voice, without a hint on an accent, was easy on the ears.

"Tomorrow at noon I'll be taking my group to see a video at the Nathaniel Dett B.M.E. Church here in Niagara Falls. Would you care to join us?" she asked.

"Wouldn't miss it for the world," I answered as we checked the map for the side street I would be looking for located in downtown Niagara Falls. "I'll see you tomorrow."

Chapter 30

The Freedom Trail

I walked in on a packed house. They were all seated and ready for the video. Every head turned to look in my direction. A little embarrassed about the whole affair, I smiled and waved at Norma. There were a couple of things that Norma had neglected to mention. The first was that there was no parking on any of the streets in the area. All the other guests, Norma included, had been let off a tourist bus that would be waiting for them while I had driven up and down the streets looking for a parking spot or a lot that could accommodate my large truck. I walked in late.....and breathless.

The second fact was that I was the only person not of color in the room. When everyone turned to look at me no one smiled. I got the distinct impression they thought I had accidentally wandered into the wrong building. Norma immediately acknowledged my presence with a smile and before she continued her presentation introduced me by name and told the group that I would be the guest speaker at their banquet in September. The group turned en masse to look my way. A few smiled, some nodded. I felt relief.

The brick church was small and cozy with each and every worshiper made to feel they had come home. A beautifully crafted Canadian-made pump organ stood on stage at the front of the room and a large television set with remote control was displayed just below the stage prepared for the video. The lights dimmed.

Although the history packed video was of interest to me, the people were a source of fascination. I watched their faces as the trials and tribulations of their ancestors unfolded before them. Unlike some fictional account of the events, this was drama in real life and touched the heart of each person watching, including mine.

While I checked out the well-worn books housed in the Norval Johnson Heritage Library, located at the back of the church, I was surprised by how many people came up to talk to me. A few brave ones asked if I was black. When I answered "no" most of the questions stopped.

The group was from Pennsylvania. For most this was their first trip to Niagara Falls and they were loving the sights on this perfect day in September and the history lesson. So was I. I waited until everyone had paid for the mementos they had chosen before approaching Norma. She was thrilled that I had stayed, apologized that there was not one spare seat on the bus and invited me on a personally guided tour of the Freedom Trail via the Underground Railroad.

"I'll buy lunch," I volunteered, "and we'll make a day of it."

It was about ten days later that Norma picked me up in front of the campground store. It would have been a crime not to get acquainted first and start the day with coffee and muffins, my downfall, from Tim Horton's Donut Shop. By the time we got back into the car we knew we were going to have a great day. We headed west on the QEW towards Fort Erie. When she pulled off the highway one kilometer (welcome to Canada) east of Bowen Road I thought something was wrong but it was the start of my history lesson.

She pointed to the open field and immediately started painting a verbal picture. "That was heavily wooded in the early 1800's and referred to as Little Africa," she said. "By the 1830's," she explained, "at all times the forest was home to approximately five hundred runaway slaves. Little Africa was the first experience with freedom that most of the slaves had and the beginning of their becoming self-sufficient. The men learned a trade. They were cutting and selling wood for the ship building trade. Each vowed to own property, something not available to them in the United States," Norma continued.

It was a short drive off Bowen Road that we visited St. John's Church where residents of the forest were not welcomed until 1880. It was almost directly across the street, and a short way down one of the paved side roads, that The Coloured Cemetery was located. We pushed opened the metal gate and walked among the few headstones, reading as we went. The grass was sparse and the old headstones askew but the cemetery looked well cared for.

We drove to the Niagara River, the designated crossing for the freedom seekers and sign posted with a Running Man landmark. It was located directly across from Buffalo, New York, the northernmost station on the Underground Railroad System. Each slave that made it that far arrived wearing a new pair of shoes so their journey could continue a little more comfortably. The shoes were provided to each by a Rochester businessman. But death awaited many.

"The Niagara River is open ended," Norma explained, "beginning in Lake Erie and ending in Lake Ontario. Quilts hanging on a line in Fort Erie indicated whether it was safe to cross. Those unfortunate enough to miss the narrow window of opportunity to land their row boats safely in Canada's Fort Erie were swept down the raging torrent. Once tipped, if they did not drown en route, they plummeted to their death over Niagara Falls. Their freedom and their lives were in the hands of strangers."

For those that made it across the river the safe house of Bertie Hall waited. Our next stop was Bertie Hall. A tunnel used by the Underground Railroad for smuggling slaves into the house was sealed when one of the sons of the Forsyth Family drowned in there. The history, along with the memorabilia in the basement, was in sharp contrast to the rest of the house. Bertie Hall is now the home of Mildred M. Mahoney Silver Jubilee Dolls' House Gallery and contains one hundred and forty miniature houses in a collection that dates from 1780 to 1980.

From Fort Erie, with a stop for lunch at a golf course clubhouse courtesy of the curator of Bertie Hall, June Spear, we toured sights a little more familiar to me. We drove to Niagara-On-The-Lake stopping at Brock's Monument, passing the Butterfly Conservatory, the Floral Clock and several wineries, before stopping at the Cemetery for Butler's Rangers and their descendants.

Colonel John Butler defected from U.S. Fort Niagara, New York to Fort George on the British side, leading a black military battalion. We did not leave the area without paying our respects to probably the greatest conductor on the Underground Railroad, Harriet Ross Tubman. A monument erected in her honor stands in the heart of Niagara-On-The-Lake.

The day was just one of the many highlights of my stay in Niagara Falls and was complete only after we stopped for homemade ice cream. It seemed like the perfect way to end the day and cement the friendship.

Chapter 31

Problems.....Solved

It was sometime during the middle of September that I started having problems with my new book Everyone's Dream Everyone's Nightmare. To the eight lowest bidders for the printing and binding of my latest, I had sent out updated Requests for Quotations since the previous thirty, sent out just before the summer started, had expired. Six of the requests went to companies in Michigan, one to Arkansas City, Kansas and one to Nashville, Tennessee, home of country music and where my heart belonged even if it was just for a temporary stay. The longer I waited for the replies the more anxious I became since campgrounds in Michigan closed mid October. Also there were no campgrounds listed in any of my camping directories anywhere close to Arkansas City. If there were thousands of dollars difference in the price for the printing and binding, I would have a real dilemma on my hands, since I would have to rent an apartment or stay in a hotel while I waited. I prayed for Nashville. When the quote from my favorite was finally received it fell somewhere in the middle of the pile. It was certainly an acceptable quote. David Prentice, who would act as my account representative had called the day he received the request to say it was being prepared and that it would be on its way in a day or so. I already felt comfortable dealing with the company whose motto is "with a touch of Southern Hospitality."

I sent him off a couple of chapters on disk along with a few pages printed directly from my Portable Stylewriter printer. David called again to say neither was acceptable. My Macintosh PowerBook contained the program ClarisWorks which their computers could not open and I needed to have the pages produced on a laser printer, with 600 dpi or better, if I wanted a sharp image. Needless to say, being mostly lingo illiterate, I first had to learn what dpi meant.

One by one I called all the printing companies in Niagara Falls and St. Catharines. Not one of them, large or small, could open a disk on ClarisWorks. I think one of the shysters offered to do the job for six dollars a page. For One thousand, five hundred and thirty-six dollars I felt I could buy a new computer, laser printer and do the job myself. I started to panic.

I called the Mac dealer in St. Catharines. The young man listened to my tale of woe. I was close to tears and could feel the stress seeping out with each word. I hated sounding so unprofessional.

"Calm down, Joei," came the sympathetic disembodied voice through the phone wires. "I'll do it for you," he offered. "As long as you don't need it in a hurry and can wait a couple of hours while the job is being done."

"What would you charge?" I asked and held my breath.

"What does Kinko charge.....seven cents a page?" he ventured a guess. "That would be okay with me."

"Bless you," I said. "What day would be convenient for you?" I asked.

Within a couple of days the job was done. I went through each page, found a few mistakes and drove the twenty-five mile round trip back into St. Catharines to have those pages redone.

On September 29, 1998 the laser printed pages for the book known as Everyone's Dream Everyone's Nightmare was sent off to the Nashville, Tennessee. That same day, directly from the graphic designer, a disk of the cover for the book was sent to Vaughan Printing.

The job was over. I took pictures of each step of the operation as the pages were boxed, wrapped and labeled and handed to the clerk at Mail Boxes, Etc. I left euphoric. A bit of depression set in long before I arrived home. "My job is finished. What do I do now," I thought.

I took the whole next day off. I relaxed, putting my feet up on the seat of my picnic table. I started reading a novel, Sole Survivor, by Dean Koontz. I wandered the campground that had now dwindled to the few diehards that would be around until the end of October before heading south for the winter. I called friends to arrange goodbye dinners or movies or weekend walks since my teacher friends were all back in school.

When I confessed to the couple parked next to me in the campground that I would be leaving in a few days and heading for Nashville and that I was still intimidated pulling my trailer a long conversation ensued. I received the best advice I had heard to date. "We've been full-timing for ten years," he said. "It takes us two years to crisscross the country. We drive for a hundred or a hundred and twenty-five miles a day and stay for a week."

I knew that I couldn't drive the eight hundred miles to Nashville but I could certainly drive a hundred miles a day. That afternoon I ordered a Triptik to Nashville supplied by the Canadian Automobile Association. I could not only follow the route easily but I could plan, in advance, which campgrounds I would stay in. I called several and made sure they were still open and would be at least until the end of October.

I wrote several articles pertaining to the promotion of my books for Writer's Guidelines & News, where I am on staff as The Road Writer. I wrote a couple of articles on nostalgia for their other magazine called Yesterday's Magazette.

I arranged to be in a campground in Sarasota, Florida for ten weeks because I felt it would be easy getting a lecture series going in a place where I was already known. I had sent out thirty letters to bookstores and women's groups where I had lectured previously and thanks to the Rotary Club in Niagara Falls I had a list of the all their clubs in North America.

While all this letter writing was going on I completed my lecture circuit in the Niagara region.

127

I purchased a deep cycle battery for my trailer from Sears. At the bank I changed some Canadian money into American money. I cleaned my trailer from one end to the other. I loaded up on groceries from my favorite Zehr's stores and filled both tanks with diesel fuel and checked the tire pressure in my truck. I called my friends to say goodbye since I would not be having a phone much longer.

On the sixteenth of October, early in the morning, I hitched up my trailer. I drove it around the campground so they could put a little air in the trailer tires. One tire seemed reluctant to accept the offer of a fresh breath but it finally worked and the tire inflated to fifty pounds of pressure. At ten-thirty I was headed out the gate. It was a short distance to the QEW heading west. Within forty-five minutes I was waiting at the border to cross over into the United States.

Chapter 32

On The Road Again

Buoyed by the fact that I was only going about ninety miles after crossing the border I felt my confidence return with each mile. It was after an easy drive down a six-lane highway with little traffic that I came to the town of North East, Pennsylvania. In checking my camping guide before leaving Niagara Falls, North East was the only open campground for the next hundred or so miles. I dared not go farther on my first day of pulling in over three months and, even at that, my respite for the night was over five miles from the highway. This was the first campground that I had called to make sure they were open.

I was happy to be off the road even though the campground did not seem to have many spots on level ground. I left my truck attached to the trailer. This was one of the few times that it worked well since my truck was oversized and overpowered and much too high for the trailer I was pulling. The trailer was relatively level and the truck was on a downhill slope.

The sun was shining. It was warm and I felt good. After attaching the various and sundry hoses I opened my awning, took out my deck chair, the latest Grisham novel and relaxed. I didn't even notice when a car pulled up. When I heard a distant "hello" I responded in kind even before I had turned around to see who had called. I watched as she approached. A dark-haired, young woman, well dressed in a navy business suit, walked towards me.

"Are you camping here?" I asked hopefully since she seemed so friendly.

"No," she replied, "the owners have an ad in the local magazine and I'm delivering a copy." "Here," she said, as she handed me a copy of Good Times put out by the Grape Coast Visitor's Bureau.

Within fifteen minutes having given her my deck chair while I sat on the trailer steps we exchanged our life histories. She purchased my first book, ordered the second and scheduled a lecture for me to at her bookstore, The Uncommon Ground, for the fifteenth of April. The six months would give her ample time to prepare and advertise. We talked for over an hour. We parted with the feeling that we had known each other all our lives. Then she was gone.

The next day, the forty-some miles of driving in Pennsylvania was very upsetting. The shoulder of the highway was littered with dead and mangled deer. At several spots two animals would be within a few feet of each other. At one point a couple of fully-grown deer ran beside the highway. With so few vehicles on the highway I slowed down to a crawl hoping they wouldn't spook and jump in front of my truck.

It was Saturday and I was happy to be driving around Cleveland without much traffic. I stopped that afternoon in Seville, Ohio. The campground was situated next to a pond complete with rowboats and fishing equipment that could be rented. After setting up I walked down to the water's edge hoping to sit on the park bench that had been provided and meditate. Within minutes I felt myself welling up with tears, lonely for the life that I had loved and shared with Paul. I knew he would have thoroughly relaxed and enjoyed an afternoon or two of fishing in a stocked pond. It all seemed like such hard work without him. I dried my eyes, went back to my camper and busied myself preparing dinner.

I really should have taken the next day off but Sundays were the best day to drive. Any reduction in the flow of traffic worked to my benefit and I had to go for it. The drive was blessedly easy even though it was overcast and breezy. I had taken three choices out of Trailer Life Camping Book and just as I passed my third choice in Jeffersonville it started to sprinkle. By the time I got off the road, thirty miles later in Lebanon, I knew I was ready for a rest.

I walked into the office. A familiar face sat behind the desk. His greeting was very enthusiastic.

"Do I know you?" I asked, "You look so familiar."

"Maybe," he replied, "I'm a Court Jester at all the Medieval Fairs. Ever go to one?"

"I volunteered at the one in Sarasota every year for five years," I said. "What a small world."

After talking for a few minutes several other campers arrived anxious to check in and settle down. I left. Bad weather brings campers in off the road early and I knew he would be too busy to talk long. Just as I finished setting up the rain became a steady stream and I was delighted to close my doors, turn on my electric heater and start dinner. The night was very cold. I needed to get farther south in a hurry.

The following day was going to be another short drive. It would take all my concentration and all my energy (since tension zaps my reserves) for the seventy-seven mile drive, most of it around Cincinnati. I was heading back into familiar territory. I knew exactly where the campground was in Walton, Kentucky just a few miles south of the Ohio border on Interstate 75 and this time I would not miss the turnoff. One experience driving around the hills of Cincinnati was more than enough.

I had no trouble until after I arrived. After painstakingly backing up my camper, something I still had not done too often, I discovered that the trailer was way off kilter and the refrigerator light was blinking at me. I needed to get a couple of boards under the right wheels. Once again the campground host helped. It didn't take long since I had to pull straight out and back straight in. This was just one of the many things, in my free spirited life, that I think of as a royal pain in the ass. It was another chilly night.

I stopped at the Flying J the following morning. This was a truck stop with cheap diesel fuel, a bay to check tire pressure, dump if necessary, wash your vehicle, eat, do laundry, take a shower, watch television in their lounge or spend the night (free of charge) in your camper or truck. I filled with diesel in preparation of an easy, easy drive. I arrived at the KOA in Elizabethtown, Kentucky around two in the afternoon and was greeted by a giant slobbering St.

Bernard whose eyes gave every indication of having consumed the entire keg of brandy that no longer hung around his neck awaiting an emergency situation.

It was after a late breakfast the next day that I decided to do some sightseeing. Abe Lincoln and I are one day apart in our birthdays and I have always felt a certain kinship to him. I went looking for his birth home in Hodgenville. The home, being a National Historic Site and well sign posted, was not difficult to find. The original log cabin has now been placed inside a Memorial Building and the tour started with a movie of what life must have been like back in 1809 in Hardin County, Kentucky.

From Abe Lincoln's home to Schmidt's Coca-Cola Museum in Elizabethtown would have been a short drive had I not gotten lost. I ended up passing by the front door several times before I realized exactly where it was. It is the world's largest, privately owned collection of memorabilia and so many of the old pieces looked familiar. I instantly reverted to my childhood when I remembered giving my father a tiny coke bottle cigarette lighter that I had wrapped in paper and put inside a small box that was put into a larger box that was put into an even larger box.

By the time I stopped for a sandwich, filled up with diesel and headed back to the camper, the rain had started. I had had a wonderful day. One more day of driving my one hundred mile per day rule and I would be in the Home of Country Music.

Chapter 33

Nashville North

Despite the wonderful day I had not slept well. I had heard so much about the Nashville traffic from so many different travelers that it had unnerved me just thinking about it and I did not rush out the next morning. I knew I wasn't going far so I left around eleven in the morning. A little south of Elizabethtown, I entered the Central Time Zone, and gained an hour. When I arrived at the Visitor's Center in Tennessee, just south of the Kentucky border, I changed my mind about where to stay. It was very early in the day when I arrived at the campground referred to as Nashville North. I looked around, checked in immediately and paid for a one- week stay.

Big mistake. Louisville is Nashville North. The Canadian border is Nashville North. This was the boonies. It was too close to Nashville for people to stop for the night and too far out of Nashville to commute. The only people who stayed were people working in the area temporarily or like me, who had made a serious error in judgment.

The day after my arrival I decided to venture into Nashville to find Vaughan Printing. Besides my fascination with country music, it was my reason for being there in the first place. Flipping through the radio stations on the way into town, I could not find one station playing country music. By the time I had run through the fifth station singing gospel music, I put in my Garth Brooks CD, and sang along at the top of my lungs. I kept one hand on the steering wheel while I conducted for Garth with the other one.

I had no trouble, thanks to the Canadian Automobile Association map of Nashville, finding Cowan Road, the street that the printing company was on. It was just a couple of right turns off Interstate 65 and when I introduced myself to the receptionist she handed me the package that was sitting upright on the filing cabinet, propped against the wall.

"These are the bluelines for your book," she said. "You can use the conference room to review them."

I took the package and slipped into the big, empty conference room. I was suddenly bursting with pride over my latest accomplishment and there was no one around who cared. Jean poked her head around the door frame and asked if I wanted a cup of coffee.

"Sure, two sugars and milk please," I answered.

After setting down the Styrofoam cup, she was gone again. It didn't take me long to get the work done. I felt a real let down as I handed back the package to her. Where was the fanfare? Where was the excitement?

I was halfway out the door when the gentleman holding it open for me asked if that was my monster truck with Florida license plates on it in their lot.

"Yes," I responded, thrilled that someone had actually acknowledged my presence.

"What are you doing in Nashville?" he asked in a friendly manner.

"My book is being printed and bound here," I told him.

Extending his hand, he said, "I'm Buddy Vaughan, has anyone given you a tour of our plant yet?"

The owner and president of the company showed me around personally. Taking me step by step through the process, we started with the paste-up boards to be photographed. I watched one high-speed line whiz past as pages were being glued into their covers. The last stop was seeing where the books were trimmed to their correct size. As we walked, he asked about my book.

The ad for Vaughan Printing in all the magazines had said "with a touch of Southern Hospitality" and I was thoroughly enjoying it. By the time I walked out of the building I was in love with Nashville and everyone living there.

With little traffic, a great city map and a slowly developing sense of direction I found my way back to the campground. I was delighted with the day's events even if I didn't have anyone to share it with.

Since I had crossed over Briley Parkway on the way to the printing company, I decided to check out the campground that I had originally wanted to stay in. According to my book it was located just off Briley Parkway, the highway that circumnavigated that part of town. Since the homeward bound traffic had started to heavy up a bit, I decided to wait until the next day.

I ventured out around noon. I had no trouble finding the Briley exit again and I knew that I would be heading in the direction of the Opryland Hotel, which was sign posted everywhere. On the drive east, then south I could see three campgrounds side by side on Music Valley Drive, the road running alongside the highway. I checked on prices and although it was a bit more money, I really wanted to be in the heart of country music city. Since it was late in the season, the tall, handsome cowboy behind the counter knew there would not be a problem finding me a spot for a month or so while I waited for the production of my new book.

Camping World, a department store for the serious RVer was located within a one-minute walk. Only a dinner theater separated the parking lots. I drove over to their lot.

"Nice truck," came the disembodied voice as I turned off the engine and stepped out onto the lot.

I looked over to see an older couple getting out of a truck as large as mine but not quite as new or growlily sounding.

"What are you pulling?" he asked.

"A twenty-two and a half foot Wanderer by Thor," I answered suddenly taking pride in the fact that I had become part of a different world complete with its own language.

"Where are you staying?" he asked.

"A little too far away," I answered. "I'll be moving next door in a few days," pointing to the Two Rivers Campground.

"What are you doing in Nashville?" he asked and I answered with a brief explanation about my writing, my new book and the fact that I would be setting up a lecture series.

Just past the double doors they turned one way, we said goodbye, and I went the other way. This was a big store and we both needed shopping room.

Back at Nashville North it took two days to discover a delightful neighbor whose husband was working in the area and she was by herself most of the day. Marjorie and I took a few excursions into Nashville to find all the bookstores listed in the telephone directory and to go to lunch. One day we just went for a drive to check out the scenery. The days passed pleasantly enough.

It was usually late afternoon when we got back to the campground after our jaunts. It was also late in October and with the time change and gaining an hour just south of Elizabethtown, Kentucky, darkness fell too early for my liking these days. When the sun went down, I was confined to the camper, feeling lonely and somewhat blue. I was anxious for the week to be over so I could move closer to familiar activities and big city life.

Chapter 34

In Love With Nashville

As much as I hated being out of the center of things, I
didn't waste any time sitting around moping. I met Lois, a cheerful ole gal, well into her seventies.
She was on her way to Florida pulling a thirty-four foot
Airstream behind a Chevy truck that was only slightly past
its prime. She was teamed up with the couple in the next
Airstream trailer, driving tandem. She had been on her own
for the past eight years. We talked until well past ten before
saying good night. She was gone when the sun came up the
next morning. I found a note taped to my door with her
winter address on it.

I found a Books-A-Million bookstore within a few
miles in Madison, Tennessee. In speaking with the manager
about having to deal with the head office and their policy on
book signings, Dawn Evans booked me for an author signing.

"I don't know when the book will be ready," I told her
outright.

"That's okay," she insisted, "all we need is a couple of
days notice."

Within a day I delivered a colored copy of my book
cover along with flyers printed on fancy paper that read SO
HOT IT'S NOT EVEN OFF THE PRESS YET.

Dawn loved my signs.

I started editing the manuscript on my 1994 travels
through Turkey. Just before darkness closed in on me for the
night I went for one last walk around the campground. I met
Don and Mary, a young couple, on their way to California.
We exchanged our life histories in a matter of minutes. When
I told them I was a writer, he became intensely interested.
He fired question after question at me and when I had to stop
to scratch at the mosquitoes biting at my legs Mary invited
me into their motorhome for coffee. I accepted without
hesitation.

"May I read you some of my poems?" Don asked.

"Sure," I responded. "I don't understand a lot of the poetry but I'd love to hear them."

I did understand his poetry. I liked them very much and told him so. Most dealt with comforting the living after the death of a loved one. The words were simple, straight from the heart and brought tears to my eyes. He seemed very relieved.

Mary explained that they had just come from a Christian Writer's Conference and had paid a small fortune to be there. He was so discouraged by the uncomplimentary remarks from a couple of the participants that he was prepared to give up writing.

"Listen only to yourself," I cautioned. "If you like it, others will too. Everything written from the heart is publishable somewhere." I chose my words carefully since my everyday language would have contained a few expletives not fit for someone who had just returned from a Christian Writer's Conference. I also explained that my first writing effort had been critiqued in that same manner just days before it was published in a two-page spread of a local, award winning newspaper.

Two cups of coffee later, something I should never do before bedtime, along with camping nightmares stories, tales from our childhood with a few jokes thrown for good measure and the evening came to a close around midnight. They both walked me back to my trailer, flashlight in hand. The thanks I got came with a hug attached.

"I actually feel like doing a little more writing right now," Don admitted. "Thank you," he said. "Thank you."

As long as I was sitting around with basically nothing to do but wait, I decided to make up order forms for my new book. I had them printed at a nearby Office Depot. I would start sending them out to friends, acquaintances, fellow travelers I had met who had given me their address and people who would no longer recognize me from a hole in the wall, it had been so long since I had been in touch. Actually, anyone whose address I had, especially those who had purchased my first book, Restless From The Start, was on my list. The flyer became a two- sided order form. The front was a black-and-white of the cover and the back gave ordering instructions in both Canadian and U.S. dollars.

Finding Office Depot wasn't difficult. Once I found Books-A-Million, everything I needed seemed to be on that same main street. It was within a block of the bookstore and they weren't busy. Fifty copies of the flyers were just a few cents more than ten copies. A hundred copies was less than half again the cost of fifty and five hundred seemed to be the best bargain. Needless to say, I'll be sending them out until the book goes into its fifth printing and in the meantime, I use the block of extra flyers to weigh down the trailer and keep it steady on the road.

As I waited for the flyers to be printed I walked all the aisles in the store checking out the fancy writing paper, new computers, printers, cell phones and the various telephone plans.

He was a rather odd looking guy as he approached me in the center aisle of Office Depot. "Are you the author?" he asked looking at me rather seriously.

"Excuse me?" I asked looking around to see if he was really talking to me.

"Are you the author?" he asked again.

"Do I know you?" I responded looking around once again to see if I was on Candid Camera or if there was someone I knew in this area, eight hundred miles from anything familiar.

"Are you the author?" he asked again, a little frustrated at not knowing what to say next.

"Yes, I guess so," I answered totally perplexed.

"You met Ray, the guy I work with, at Camping World a few days ago and he sent me over here to find you," he said, giving me a straight answer.

"How did he know I was here?" I asked.

"He just came on duty and recognized your truck in the lot," he answered feeling a little more comfortable that he had obviously found the right person.

139

"Did you ask everyone in Office Depot before you got to me?" I asked rather amused with the entire situation.

"No, you were the only one I asked," he answered.

"How did Ray describe me that you knew it was me," I asked, my curiosity getting the best of me.

"He said just look for the tall pretty lady," he answered innocently.

"Oh God, I'm going to love Nashville," I thought.

Red Bailey, forty something, short and round with a mass of carrot-red hair and wearing a striped, too tight, T-shirt and shorts lead me back to the offices of Home Depot, located right next door, where they both worked on the switchboard. In between telephone calls we talked.

Red and I made a date to meet for lunch at one of his favorite Chinese restaurants.

Chapter 35

Ecstasy

I was in ecstasy. That was the only way to describe my three weeks at the Two Rivers Campground in Nashville, Tennessee. With the help of my trusty CAA map and the telephone directory I found addresses for all the bookstores in and around Nashville. I visited Davis-Kidd, a Tennessee chain with a jam-packed calendar of events going on each month. I picked up the free newspaper listing all the local happenings in the various districts around the city. Bookstar, owned by Barnes & Noble, is housed in an old movie theater, marquee and all, and I could actually visualize my name up there in lights for the whole world to see. That particular bookstore took a little time to find since street names had a habit of changing after crossing a major intersection. Barnes & Noble in Brentwood needed highway driving but I found it also.

I attended writers' groups, one at a local library and another at Davis-Kidd. I went to poetry readings every Friday night at Books-A-Million in Madison. I found a Toastmaster group where they insisted that I do the first speech in the beginner's manual called 'The Icebreaker'. I had done this speech and others so often it became second nature. At that meeting I formed an instant attachment to dark-haired, soft-spoken Wanda Pickens. At coffee, after the meeting, I met her husband Gene.

I made friends in the campground as well. Barb and Gerry Downs were parked directly across from me. When Barb pulled in behind the wheel of a Weirs International Diesel, I had to comment. Man-oh-man was I impressed. Barb, fair-haired and in her early sixties was friendly and easy to talk to, especially about driving. She explained that her truck, as big as it was, was much easier to drive and turned in smaller quarters than my Ford F-250. I found that out on a number of occasions when they invited me to join them on several day trips.

It was bright and sunny but cool on the last day of October when the three of us went to the Hermitage Plantation, home of the seventh President of the United State, Andrew Jackson. Almost all the furnishings in the mansion are original and a complete restoration has returned the home to its initial appearance. With so much ground to cover we did not spend a lot of time indoors. We walked the garden but there was not much to see. An early frost had killed many of the vegetables and they had been left in the field to rot. Not a pretty sight. We saw the tomb, a monument built for his beloved wife Rachel. Jackson was buried beside her after his death in 1845. We walked through the Tulip Grove, residence of Andrew Jackson Donelson, Rachel's nephew and President Jackson's secretary and strolled to the edge of the property where the Springhouse provided refrigeration for dairy products.

It was cold by the time we left and just beginning to get dark. We were back on Music Valley Drive, very close to home, when Barb asked if I wanted to stop for dinner or should they drop me off at home.

"Dinner sounds great," I answered, "where were you thinking of going?"

"Have you ever been to the Sante Fe Steakhouse?" she asked, just as we were approaching.

"As a matter of fact, they have several in Sarasota and they were always so crowded I've never been. I'm game," I said as she swung into their parking lot.

We waited with the engine idling while it cooled and, as usual, Gerry got out and put yellow blocks under the two back wheels. I left my camera and a handful of Hermitage brochures sitting on my seat as I opened the door and backed down the two steps.

Although the restaurant was crowded with patrons and staff in costume, the first we had realized that it was Halloween, it didn't take us long to be seated. Signs on each table indicated that the special of the day was Jack Daniels steak.

"Oh, that sounds great," said Barb, "but I'm driving, I don't think I should have liquor."

"Go ahead, Barb," I responded, "it's just the flavor, I'm sure the booze burns off in the open flame."

"What can I get you to drink?" asked the waiter who suddenly appeared carrying three place settings.

"What do you have?" asked Barb and the young man went through a list of various beers, on tap and in the bottle. He mentioned red, white or rose wine, Texas Tea and soft drinks.

"Texas Tea sounds nice," said Barb, "I'll have some of that, no ice, please."

"I'll have the same with ice," said Gerry.

"I'll have ice water," I responded.

While we yakked about what a pleasant day it had been with a couple of the latest jokes I had heard thrown in, the waiter brought the drinks.

Barb took a sip. She wrinkled up her nose a bit and took another sip. "How's yours, Gerry?" she asked.

Mine's okay," he responded.

"What's wrong?" I asked.

"This has some strange spices in it," she said, taking another couple of sips. "You try it," she said handing me a fresh straw. She took another sip while I took the paper wrapping off the straw.

"Strange spices, my ass," I said, "that's Tequila."

"No, it's Texas Tea," she said adamantly, waving at a waiter, even though he wasn't our waiter.

"What's in Texas Tea?" she asked.

"All white liquors," he responded, "gin, vodka, rum, tequila. Can I get you something else," he asked as she pushed the glass over to Gerry who was quietly enjoying the booze, the humor and my giggling.

"And you didn't want the Specialty of the House because it was broiled in bourbon," I responded. "You'll probably be too drunk to taste it anyway. I'll drive home," I volunteered quickly, knowing full well, I would be panic stricken behind the wheel of that monster.

Am I ever going to let her live that one down? I don't think so. As a matter of fact I mention it to them in every letter.

With only a mile or so to drive home, we made it with no problem.....and with Barb behind the wheel. We arrived home a little after eight. I turned the television set on and promptly fell asleep. A full day of fresh air does that to me. I awoke in time to change my clothes, head out the door, start my truck and hope that I didn't disturb too many people since it was around eleven in the evening. A couple of miles down the road I walked into the theater to listen to Ernest Tubb's Midnight Jamboree. The radio program has been on the air for some fifty years and I was in the audience listening to the guest host, Cajun Country and Western singer, Jimmie C. Newman. I might as well have been five years old sitting on the floor in front of the radio with the rest of my family listening.

Ecstasy, that is the only way to describe my three weeks at the Two Rivers Campground in Nashville, Tennessee.

144

Chapter 36

Natchez Trace

It was about ten days later that I called Vaughan Printing to find out how my book was progressing.

"Still on schedule," answered Jean, "but David Prentice is in now and he really wants to talk to you."

"Joei," came the sound of an enthusiastic voice through the phone wires, "when am I going to get to meet you in person?" he asked.

"I have an appointment at the bank on Friday," I said, "how about coffee?"

"Wonderful, looking forward to it. See you then," he replied.

Friday morning was a sad one. I said goodbye to my neighbors Barb and Gerry, who were heading to Texas via the Natchez Trace. We sat outside on our deck chairs and had coffee together before they started the cleaning and gathering process. I left them to finish doing their stuff and returned to my camper. I retrieved my bankbook and Certificate of Deposit information from the bowels of my handbag that I kept stuffed in a back closet, making sure I had my driver's license and passport for identification. I wolfed down breakfast. When I left around ten thirty, they were just pulling out with Barb sitting tall behind the wheel. We honked and waved at each other.

I had already been lost in downtown Nashville once but I knew I could find the bank after going to Vaughan Printing. Since so many of the inner city streets are one way only with so many bridges that don't go back to where I wanted to go, I went to Vaughan first.

Two young male executives, one sitting, one standing, were talking by the front door. The blond seated one looked my way, "Can I help you?" he asked.

"I'm here to see David Prentice," I said.

"The Gypsies came and took him," he responded.

"Great," I retorted, "what did you have to pay them for that service. You must be David," I said, putting my hand out which he promptly accepted and shook.

After showing me his office, which he uses more for storage than for business, he lead me back to the Conference Room, a place I was already familiar with.

It was a most enjoyable hour and a half without benefit of the promised cup of coffee. We talked about his traveling, bits and pieces of information about his family and the printing business. We talked about my plans of traveling and lecturing and he loved my promotional ideas. He also loved the book cover. "Everyone who sees the cover comments on it," he said. "I keep a copy of it on my desk. Dynamite cover"

"Any ideas about how I can get a distributor for it?" I asked over an hour after the start of the conversation.

"Leave it with me," he said. "I'll ask around."

By the end of the tete-a-tete, I was as enthusiastic as David and knew he would find a distributor for me.

Thanks to the Assistant Manager at the Southtrust Bank, the transfer of funds from my Sarasota account took no time at all and I was on my way again, heading home. On the way back to the campground I located the Shoney's restaurant where the Toastmasters' meeting would be held that night. I made a mental note of the cross street. It did not seem to be an attractive part of town and there were not a lot of stores in the area where I could wile away a couple of hours. I decided to drive the twelve miles back to my camper for dinner.

Surprise. Barb and Gerry were parked in their usual spot. They were sitting outside, under their awning, and waved as I pulled up and parked.

"What happened?" I asked, not terribly concerned since they both seemed to be all right.

"We were on the highway right over there," Barb said pointing over the hedges to Briley Parkway in direct line with Two Rivers, "and we had a blowout. Didn't even know what happened until several people pointed and we pulled over to check. We drove slowly to Gallatin Road, found a tire dealer and they replaced the tire. The tread came off and was flapping around. Can you believe it?" she asked not expecting an answer. "You'd think it was a retread. It tore up the undercarriage of the trailer," she said. "Come see. We've called Goodyear and our insurance company," she said. "They're going to fix it next door," pointing to Cullum and Maxey, "but it'll take awhile. They have to order the parts. So we're back."

"Sorry about this nasty development, but I'm glad your back," I said giving them both a hug.

It was a couple of days later that there was a knock on my door. "We're going to drive down the Natchez Trace for about fifty miles," said Barb, "want to go?"

I inhaled my breakfast, dressed and was out the door in fifteen minutes flat. It took over an hour of driving from the east side of Nashville to the west side via Briley Parkway. Finding the beginning of our adventure route also took some doing but once on the Natchez Trace Parkway, it was scenery of unmistakable beauty. The traffic was extremely light on that bright, crisp, cool day in early November and no trucks are permitted on that Parkway which made traveling and sightseeing all the more enjoyable.

At its start The Trace was probably a series of hunters' paths that slowly formed a trail from Mississippi over the low hills into the valley of Tennessee. By the 1730's the French knew it well enough to map the trading route.

We stopped at every lookout point to see the changing colors of the leaves or a bridge or to read a plaque or check a trail. We walked a mile or so down the Old Trace just to enjoy the serenity and to stretch our legs. We had to do some fancy footwork to avoid what the horses had left on the path. We went into the National Park Service office at Leipers Fork to talk to the Rangers and, of course, to use the rest rooms. The facilities were not open to the public so we picked up a couple of brochures and didn't linger long. The information was on volunteering for the Park Service. I perused them and we were on our way.   At Fly we turned off and headed for Columbia.

The fresh air and exercise had worked its magic. We all had the feeling that our stomachs thought our throats had been cut. We were starving. There was an all-you-can-eat lunch buffet at the Steak Sizzler. Their country fried chicken was fabulous along with every type of salad imaginable, corn on the cob, potatoes made any way you would like, pudding, cakes, pies, a gelatin dessert in various flavors, ice cream sundaes with sprinkles, syrup, nuts and cherries. We ate too much and too fast and had to loosen our belts so we could relax over coffee and tea and let things settle down. When asked if we would like anything else. I responded with "yes, I need a crane to get me up off the seat."

We drove back slowly. We stayed on the main road and discovered that a Saturn plant was on route. We were too late for an organized tour but we wandered through the rooms turning on each of the television sets to see a video of the various functions in the plant. At the end I asked if they gave samples. Obviously they had heard that one a few too many times, and it produced a smile only in Barb and Gerry. "No," was the only response from the receptionist.

We arrived home around six. A box weighing several pounds, stuffed full of mail arrived from Sarasota. Barb and Gerry got a package from their post office box service in Livingston, Texas. We said goodbye quickly, both anxious to see what goodies the mail held.

Chapter 37

Some Good News, Some Bad News

Rats. The Florida based RV dealership where I had purchased my trailer was pulling more shenanigans. The letter I received, amongst the pile of other mail, was from the repairman who had come out to the campground in Milton, Ontario to repair the drip behind my shower the previous May.

"After several long distance calls and letters, your company has now refused to pay any of it (copy of bill enclosed). If you can help I would appreciate it. If you have to pay the bill, we will make some kind of settlement," the letter stated.

I could feel my blood pressure rising to the boiling point. Fuming, I turned on my computer and went to work immediately. I wrote to the repairman asking him to be patient and that I would get him his money. I wrote to the Florida based RV dealer attaching a copy of the letter from the repairman along with a copy of the letter I would be sending to the head office of Thor in California. Head office got copies of everything as well and it was all sent out within a day. What is that expression about Hell hath no fury......

It didn't take long. I received a letter from the repairman telling me he had been paid directly by Thor California soon after receiving my letter. He thanked me. I received a letter from Thor California advising me that they had enrolled me in their travel club protection plan free of charge. I received nothing from the RV dealer in St. Augustine, Florida.

It was in the dead of night, only hours later that a loud thud awakened me. With my heart pounding I bolted upright. The wind had picked up and I became instantly aware of the crackling branches. I had to think through a foggy brain if I had taken in my awning. I peeked outside. The awning was retracted. By the lights burning on the electrical poles I could see branches strewn all over the ground, some big ones, that would have needed close to gale force winds to bring down. I assumed that one of the large ones had crashed down, landing on my roof and waking me with a start. I hoped it hadn't done any damage. Checking out the roof situation would have to wait until morning but I never did go back to sleep. When the rain started, driven by that same gusty wind, it battered the side of my trailer that was suddenly feeling extremely flimsy. I closed all the ceiling hatches and made sure the windows were shut. I tried to relax and read but couldn't concentrate.

At first light, the rain took a short break. I went outside to check the damage. I climbed up to see what had happened to my roof but the branch that hit it toppled over the side and dented one of the ripples in the aluminum just below my bedroom window. There were lots of leaves and a few twigs on top of the trailer, nothing more. If that was the only problem, it was not serious. Nothing was broken, just a little dented. Hopefully it was something only I noticed.

When the rain started again, I went inside. It didn't let up for hours. It stayed dark and ominous most of the day. By early afternoon I couldn't stand the confinement and ventured outdoors. I got into my truck, drove to the local grocery store four miles away, and shopped for a couple of hours, checking out ingredients on products that I would never dream of buying. It killed the afternoon effectively and by the time I returned to the campground the rain had abated and a few new tenants had taken up temporary residence.

A large, Class A motorhome was parked beside me. Plastic sheeting covered the enormous passenger's front window and both occupants were outside. He was attaching all the hoses and things and she was sitting on a deck chair playing with a cell phone.

"What happened?" I asked.

"We were shopping at Camping World in Bowling Green, Kentucky," he said. When we came out a giant tree limb had come down and went straight through it. Could hardly move the damn thing," he said. "Took the help of several people to remove it. We can't drive it any farther. Pieces of the window keep falling inside," he continued.

"What are you going to do now?" I asked.

"We called our insurance company. They have arranged for a local guy to fix it, but we have to wait for them to order the window. We might be here a week or more," he said.

"Well, I'm here awhile myself, if you need anything please let me know," I said before returning to my camper.

It was the next day when she asked where the closest supermarket was.

"About four miles away," I said. "How are you going to get there?" I asked.

"We'll take a cab," he answered very matter-of-factly.

"I've got a bunch of errands to run. If you don't mind going to Wal-Mart, Sam's Club and Books-A-Million, I'll take you," I volunteered.

"We need lots of groceries," he said.

"I've got a big truck," I answered. "I'm sure it'll handle what you need. Would love the company."

We had a wonderful shopping day and treated ourselves to a McFlurry at McDonald's before stopping for groceries. Before the week was over, they were on their way. Apparently the window had been ordered, was now in stock and the local repairman had shelved a few other customers so they could work on getting this couple back on the road to Florida. They came over to thank me and to say goodbye.

I was getting itchy to be on the road myself and called Vaughan Printing to find out when my books would be ready. It would still be about ten days but the good news was that David had found a distributor for my new book. It was a couple of days later that I got together with the president of Premium Press America. Before the day was out we had an agreement.

While I waited, I went to all the local bookstores to set up lectures or book signings starting the third week of March.

I booked Barnes & Noble, Bookstar, Books-A-Million and hoped that in the end David-Kidd and Bookland would come through. I guaranteed the manager of each store a definite lecture date and time and I would be sending them a confirming letter as soon as I arrived in Florida.

I also said goodbye, for the second time, to Barb and Gerry. Although different couples came and went and there always seemed to be someone to talk to, I missed them even before they were through the gate.

It was on the seventeenth of November, when I called David, that he told me to bring my camera and come on down. I could take pictures of my book in the various stages of completion. I left right after the phone call.

I took pictures of the gorgeous cover, stacked in one pile. I took pictures of the signatures, sitting on several pallets on the floor. I checked over the first couple of books that are done by hand. David took a picture of me with my new book standing beside various piles of work yet to be done.

What hit me was.....disappointment. All that work. All that waiting. All that dreaming. It was all over. It looked "like a real book" except, of course, that it had my name on it. I also knew that the real work was about to start. The promotion of a book is an endless chore and I had already been through it once.

When I returned to the campground, I tried calling a few friends so someone else would be excited for me and help get my enthusiasm going. I couldn't reach anyone at home.

I arranged to pick up approximately one thousand books the next day and had the balance of two thousand three hundred and eighteen delivered to Premium Press. I arranged for a book signing at Books-A-Million for that Friday.

What surprised me most, besides the fact that friends from Toastmasters and the poetry club came over to buy books, was that Restless From The Start, my first book and not nearly to the caliber of the second, sold as well as Everyone's Dream Everyone's Nightmare.

The following morning, I hitched up my trailer, arranged with the campground for my return in March and headed south.

Chapter 38

My Friend Red Bailey

What happened at my luncheon date with Red Bailey, you ask? For those romantics, and for my family and friends who would be thrilled, not to mention relieved, I might add, if I met someone special, sorry. I must confess it was a pleasant treat to be with a male much younger than myself, who had never been married and whose conversation did not slip to former spouses that had done him wrong and to children whom he was not in touch with. The conversation was filled with travel experiences, since he had just returned from Pidgeon Forge and the kinds of foods we both relished. An easier conversation might have been what foods we didn't enjoy. His song writing and jokes, mostly one liners that we howled at, interspersed an already lively conversation. His hour lunch break flew by and before he returned to work, we promised we would do that again. And we did.

Red picked me up at the campground that Saturday. We drove around to the stars' homes. Hank Snow's red bus was still parked beside his house. We saw Vince Gill's home from a distance and when we stopped in front of Jeanne Seeley's home there were people there that Red knew. He stopped to talk. "The well-dressed chatty one was Ms. Seeley's manager," Red informed me after we left.

The rest of that day was spent on a horse farm outside the city, the direction of which I could not even venture a guess. Red purchased a couple of packages of lemon-filled vanilla cookies at the corner store. I thought he was kidding when he said they were for the animals, but he wasn't. There were a few horses. Several camels came loping over as soon as they saw the car go into the field. Red warned me not to get too close, "they get very aggressive and want more then their share of the cookies." A few donkeys sauntered over for their share of the goodies, one of them only two months old and absolutely adorable. Five emus were running around the field being chased by a Blue Heeler, a breed of dog that I had never heard of before. The dog nipped at the heels of the large, seemingly panicked birds. When the cookies were gone, so were we. The animals, particularly the camels, kept sticking their noses into our pockets and had no qualms about putting their heads through the open window of the car, as we were trying to make our getaway.

Sunday was another day off for Red. He picked me up early, even though it was raining. We spent the morning walking around the splendid Opryland Hotel. They were in the throws of decorating for Christmas. I took pictures as diminutive hot air balloons were hung from the ceiling with wires and enormous trees, covered with tinsel and lights, were finished with tiny gift wrapped boxes and miniature teddy bears sporting plaid ribbons around their necks. I took pictures of the indoor waterfalls and of the boat that cruised the waterways. We watched the spinning and dancing water fountains while carols played in the background.

By the time we had walked in and out of almost every store, looked at all the windows and took an entire roll of film, we were ravenous. We went to Fuddruckers for a burger and fries lunch, another favorite of Red's.

When we passed a garage sale, he asked if I minded if we stopped.

"I love garage sales," I gushed and was out the door as soon as he pulled to the curb. In between visiting The Parthenon, an exact replica of the one in Athens, Greece, shopping at Office Max and Sam's Club, we stopped at every garage sale. The entire weekend just slipped by.

The day I picked up twenty-five boxes of my new book, Everyone's Dream Everyone's Nightmare and could not reach any of my friends that would have been very excited with me, I called Red. I asked if he would like to meet me for dinner, "I really need a little celebration," I confessed.

"Sure," he said enthusiastically. "Meet you in Home Depot's parking lot and we'll go from there," he said.

155

That night we went to Uncle Dan's, famous for their extra crispy, finger licking good, southern fried chicken served with gravy, french fried potatoes, potato salad and/or coleslaw. It was delicious and the portion large enough to choke a horse, as the saying goes......but we finished it all anyway.

The conversation was a little subdued. We both knew I would be leaving in a day or so. The following day, Red worked late and did not show up at my book signing. That dinner was our last. It had been a wonderful stay in Nashville, much of it, thanks to my friend Red Bailey.

Chapter 39

Birmingham, Alabama

It was an uneventful drive south on Interstate 65. I had written out directions to the Good Sam Campground in Gardendale, Alabama approximately one hundred and eighty-five miles south of Nashville and twelve miles north of Birmingham. That was where I was planning to park for the night. I got off at the correct exit. I turned the proper way, crossed over US-31 to Moncrief Road and less than mile down the road found a muddy, unkempt little campground with trailers so close to each other, you could put your hand out and touch your next door neighbor. That thought certainly did not appeal to me. The sign near the entrance read Palomino camping. Added to my misery was the fact that the campground was adjacent to a cemetery. I pulled in, drove around the outer perimeter and pulled back out onto the road. Surely, this could not be the Good Sam campground mentioned in the book. I ended up a couple of miles away in the parking lot of a supermarket intending to go through my guide again.

There were a couple of people working on the ATM machine outside the bank. I approached, camping book in hand. The thirty year old, dark-haired guy sitting behind the wheel of a telephone truck, was my perfect choice of person to ask for directions, since I assumed he was well acquainted with the area. He had no idea where the Good Sam park was but did know the one that I had just come through. He called the telephone number listed and got exact directions to the one I wanted. Following the step-by-step directions, I ended up back at the Palomino. I didn't want to embarrass myself by going through it again and then backing out again. I booked in for one day.

I set up my camper and before setting out all my little niceties, I got out my Trailer Life and Woodall's to see where I could go the next day. My plans were to hopefully arrange book signings at the four Books-A-Million stores and to call on their head office, located in an industrial park area of Birmingham. I definitely had to stay someplace in the vicinity. There was only one other campground. It was a KOA, much more expensive and not nearly as conveniently located. I decided I would grin and bear it as long as necessary and not a second more. After realizing that I would be there awhile, I went back up to the office. Many of the residents and Martha, the owner's wife and partner, who had checked me in, were seated around a picnic table talking. I was given a warm welcome and immediately included in the conversation. They certainly seemed to be a friendly lot.

Up before dawn, I had to wait for the office to open before I could go looking for a branch of the AAA. I needed a city map and they were my best and cheapest source. Barney Booth, owner of the campground and on duty early, called AAA for their closest location. It was a long way off, but easy to find, I was told. I was told wrong.

Firstly I didn't realize that "a long way off" would be over thirty miles and well south of the city center. After driving fifteen miles or so, I turned around and ended up in downtown Birmingham where streets seem to go in circles, with too many going one way or the other but never both. Somehow I ended up coming back to the same spot over and over and becoming extremely aggravated.

I pulled into a nearly empty city lot. In the small office three men had gathered. I asked if anyone knew where the AAA office was. One man tried to describe its location, complete with totally unfamiliar street names. I needed a map of where he was trying to tell me to go and, of course, if I had had a map of where the office was, I wouldn't have needed the office in the first place. Acknowledging my frustration, he finally said, "I'm going right by the place, follow me."

I thanked him. It turned out I was following a garbage truck. Fortunately for me he made no stops or pickups on the way. He led me directly to it and stopped in front of the building and pointed. There was a parking spot, with fifteen minutes worth of time left on the meter, right in front of the door. I pulled in. Parked. I ran into the office, membership card in hand. I took a map of Birmingham, Montgomery and Dothan. I was back in my vehicle with minutes to spare. I used the time left on the meter to study the map.

I found my way back onto Interstate 65, heading south, and got off at the exit where the Hoover Commons store was located. Within a few minutes the manager had booked a lecture for mid-March and had purchased five of each book. I was elated.

Buoyed by my instant success, I headed north and found the Wildwood Store without much trouble. The manager wouldn't be in until noon the next day. At least I had found it and it would be easier the next day. I returned to the campground, a definite spring in my step.

I planned my strategy for the next day and had a letter prepared for the head office since I discovered, thanks to the map, it was close to the Wildwood store. When I finished my computer work for the day, I went for a walk in the cemetery, which seemed to have a lot of people just strolling. Close to the entrance there was a long, narrow tombstone that seemed to be beckoning. I went to look. It contained the names of two girls and one boy, all born on the same day and all died on the next. The next one also belonged to another tiny child. I stopped looking at tombstones and just walked on the paths that skirted the place.

The grassy area was covered with sandy mounds of anthills, larger and far more deadly looking than the ones I had seen in Florida. I dared not step anyplace close. The word 'fire ant' now strikes fear in my heart. When I wore myself out walking the paths, I returned to the campground and joined the group sitting at the picnic table near the office and shared my day's events with them. It was all very exciting.

I left early the next morning and although I had been hoping to have a conversation and personally hand the letter and copy of my new book over to an account executive for Books-A-Million, no such luck. I had to leave it with the receptionist who assured me it would get to the right person. I left a little disheartened.

Over coffee and a lemon poppy seed muffin, I waited for the manager at the Wildwood store. Since the 'head office fiasco' had taken no time at all, I had a couple of hours to wait. I had already wandered the shopping center, had consumed a light lunch before going back to the bookstore to kill another hour or so. Renea Jones, the manager, was very efficient with her time when she arrived. We sat on a couple of the comfortable lounge chairs in the middle of the aisle near the center cash and the information and ordering counter and made both lecture and book signing plans. Before the half-hour was up I was booked into both of the stores she managed. I would be doing a lecture on Self-Publishing and Promotion from one to three in the Wildwood Store and a lecture on Alaska from four to six at the other store. She preferred to wait until my lecture in March to purchase the books. Rats.

Before getting back on the highway, I noticed that traffic was starting to back up. Although it was relatively early, I chose to head back to the campground, doing a little grocery shopping and filling up with diesel on the way. My latest CD of Jolson tunes accompanied me and played just loud enough to kill any chance of the person in the next vehicle hearing me sing along.

When I returned to my spot, I turned on the news and discovered why traffic was backed up so early. The driver of a car had admitted to the police that, "he was sick to death of giving those damn truck drivers the right of way." He had cut off a truck that veered into the middle lane hitting a tractor trailer that, in turn, had smashed into a van that hit the guardrail. Four people had been killed. That news was coupled with a middle of the night, high-speed chase on that same highway. A young man had stolen a car in Gainesville, Florida. During the chase, at over a hundred miles an hour, around two the previous morning, he had hit the guardrail and burst into flames.

I turned off the news and went back up to the office to join my friends. The conversation at the table, not nearly as exciting, was far more palatable.

The next day, I found the last of the bookstores on the east side of Birmingham. Again I had to wait for the manager. Again I had a cup of coffee and a lemon poppy seed muffin. Hunched over the sink in the restroom, I was trying to be discrete about picking the poppy seeds out of my teeth, when the door opened.

She was nicely dressed and wearing a name tag, so I asked "Your not the manager, are you?"

"No," she replied, "I'm the Special Events Coordinator."

"Well," I said, "so much for a good first impression. I'm here to talk to you."

She laughed. "They're my favorite too," she volunteered. "I'll wait for you at the information desk."

In a matter of minutes I was booked for a lecture and book signing and was back on the road heading for home. My job in Birmingham was done. That evening I said goodbye to Barney and Martha.

"You can't leave yet," said Martha, "tomorrow is Thanksgiving. You can't be with strangers on a holiday. My sister Louise asked me to invite you to dinner."

I was stunned. Of course I said "yes" and the holiday was a wonderful traditional one starting with prayers. I brought a dessert but it paled by comparison with what was already on the table. The center of it almost caved in from the sheer weight of it all. A large turkey with all the trimmings, a full ham with all the trimmings, at least a half dozen different salads, potatoes, yams, green beans with slivered almonds, corn and a bunch of things I didn't have room to try graced the table. The desserts lined the kitchen counter near the sink.

Except for me, a total stranger to most, the house was filled with family members. There were nieces, nephews, a stepdaughter from a former marriage and the group that I arrived with. Most left right after dinner, particularly the ones with small children. Barney returned to work. I helped with the clean up, which consisted mostly of containerizing the leftovers and throwing out the used paper products. When it was all done Martha, Louise and I went walking around the neighborhood. It was either going for a long walk or leaving my pants unzipped which does not make a pretty picture. We all voted for the walk. It was after dark when Martha drove me back to the campground. Barney had been there for hours checking in people that had chosen to be on the road on that holiday.

I stayed the next day, after hearing that the heaviest accident day of the year was the day after Thanksgiving. The news had already given me a taste of Birmingham road rage. I didn't want to risk being another statistic.

It was the following morning that I discovered that I was planted on a bit of a hill and had parked slightly askew. I had trouble hitching up and had backed up and pulled forward so many times I was starting to curse. To be honest I cursed every time I had to back up and pull forward more than once. This time I was starting to curse out loud and worried about talking to the devil so close to the cemetery. Just as half the male population within earshot headed my way hoping to direct me, the trailer snapped into place. I waved to them all. It was a few minutes later that I drove through the gate.

Chapter 40

A Close Call

It was a tedious and exhausting trip setting up special events in all the major stores while heading south. After leaving Birmingham I camped in a familiar spot that night in Troy, Alabama. It was the same spot I had chosen on my way back from Alaska in 1995 and thankfully it was right on the main road and as clean and friendly as I had remembered. I called on the Barnes & Noble in Montgomery and left, for their perusal, a condensed autobiography, a blurb about each of my books and colorful flyers. At the Books-A-Million in that town I received a very warm welcome. They were in the middle of another book signing with Jeff Barganiere, author of the recently published Slash Brokers and while I waited for the manager I spoke with Jeff. He is a charming, handsome, well-spoken lawyer from Wetumpka, Alabama and before our conversation ended we had exchanged autographed copies of our books.

By the time my meeting with the manager and special events coordinator was underway I was in an exceptionally good mood and most of the headache that I had awakened with was gone. They booked a lecture and bought three of each of my books to keep on hand for advertising purposes.

I booked a lecture in Dothan, Alabama with a manager that was totally indifferent and kept me waiting over an hour without even a hint of an explanation or apology, before saying "sure, fine with me" and walked away without even making a note of the date and time.

A couple of days later I did the same in Tallahassee with their four bookstores. I quite liked that city. I spent several days driving around Florida's capital and on a couple of occasions passed a rather serene-looking city park with a walking path around a small lake. I decided, since it was such a beautiful day, I would get some exercise and walk around the lake a couple of times. I pulled into their parking lot and changed from my sandals into my tennis shoes. There were just a few people out since it was the middle of a working day and I ended up falling into step with another walker, a woman about my own age, also dressed in shorts and a T-shirt. While we walked, we carried on a conversation. She was headed to England on a vacation and was delighted when I was able to fill her in on some spots that were not to be missed. When we arrived back at the parking lot, ready to call it quits for the day, a local television crew had just moved into the lot, complete with large, shoulder-held camera and microphone. Being the overly curious type, I had to find out what was going on. A bit camera shy and needing to get back to her laundry, sorting and packing, Audrey excused herself, wished me luck and left. I approached the young woman reporter. "May I ask you a question?" she asked, keeping the microphone down at her side

"What's it about?" I answered, wanting to stay noncommittal until I confirmed the subject matter.

"We are approaching Thanksgiving," she said, "and I was wondering if you could tell us about an interesting holiday experience you've had."

She gave me a moment to think about it and I responded with the story of Thanksgiving at the campground in Gardendale, Alabama, since my mind only thinks in recent events and not ancient history. After she turned off the microphone, she said it would be shown around Christmas time so if I was on television in the Tallahassee area, I never knew. I enjoyed the interview. It gave me a little experience being "The Star". I silently thanked Toastmasters and returned to the campground feeling on top of the world with a fascinating new story to tell my friends.

In Gainesville I went back to the dreary job of setting up lectures. I did the same in Ocala.

With all the driving I had done while pulling a trailer I had only one close call. Needless to say, however, one is more than enough. I was about halfway between Ocala and Sarasota heading south on Interstate 75. Directly in front of me a tractor trailer blew a rear tire. I was close enough to hear the explosion and in direct line of fire of all the flying debris. It took a split second for instinct to kick in. I had always heard that running over the tread of a steel belted radial would shred my tires and possibly ruin the undercarriage of my truck and/or trailer. There was no time to evaluate if that was true or not. I swerved into the right lane, avoiding much of the debris that was still rolling around the roadway. Immediately, I veered back into lane number two, my leg dangling in mid air, having taken my foot off the gas pedal. I was trying desperately to refrain from jamming on my brakes, which would probably jackknife my trailer. I just steered. The truck driver pulled off to the soft shoulder while several cars behind him did the same. I cruised past them all, maintaining a forward direction and had finally slowed down enough to gently apply the brakes. I too pulled over to the soft shoulder. I took a few deep breaths, watched as all the cars got back onto the highway and did the same, shaking from the experience.

A Flying J, my favorite fully equipped gas station, was just a few exits away according to the billboards. I drove the rest of the way slowly, my fingers gripping the steering wheel for dear life and pulled into it to fill my gas tank and to give my truck and trailer the once over. I took a much needed breather for a half hour or so.

The rest of the journey was without incident and I was relieved to arrive alive at Sun-N-Fun in Sarasota. I had been through the place as a visitor with my friend Mary the previous year. After scrutinizing fourteen or fifteen campgrounds, between Bradenton and Venice, looking for a suitable place for me to camp for the winter Margaret Drew and Mary had insisted that I book into that park. I had paid for ten weeks in advance and I was now booking in a few days early.

I was greeted with a hug by Rick 'the Trickster' Cusolito who was now working the desk at Sun-N-Fun. Rick, a former circus performer turned singer/disk jockey, and I belonged to the same Toastmaster club.

"Our Christmas party is tonight at my house," said Rick. "The group will just die if you show up."

"Well," I announced, "I guess I'll just have to kill'em then. I'll be there. Let me go get set up."

I have disliked Sarasota since I got stranded there, but with a start like this, how could it miss. Perhaps living in a campground with all new and friendly people around will be more fun than living in that dreaded condo, I thought.

I thought wrong.

Chapter 41

Total Frustration

I followed the golf cart to the spot that had been reserved for me. I pulled down a narrow, bumpy road and was expected to back in. I tried. I tried again and then a third time. The front wheels of the truck kept getting hung up on boulders that had been parked in the corner of each lot to show where one property ended and the next began. I couldn't maneuver around cars that were parked too far out in the roadway. I worried about hitting something that would damage my truck and would certainly create an enemy of my neighbor if I left tire marks on his newly planted one foot by one foot square front lawn. The young fellow waiting patiently in the cart, supposedly experienced, then gave it his best effort. After several attempts he backed it in for me and stopped. I thanked him before he went off to his next project.

The services were not accessible. I backed up the trailer so I could reach the electricity and the water supply. My sewer hose would have needed an additional forty feet if I stayed in that spot. I pulled forward a few inches to try and make do and the trailer was suddenly lopsided. Had I been a drunken sailor riding the high seas the angle of my trailer would have been perfect. I stepped outside and looked around to see what I could try next. That's when I noticed the camping site next to mine. There stood a giant mound of sandy rubble reminisce of a dreaded anthill. My goose bumps got goose bumps of their own and, in my mind, the hives were already starting to break out. I walked the half-mile back to the office.

"The spot they want me to use just won't do," I said to the girl that was now standing behind the desk.

"Let me see what they have in the computer in your price range," she said politely and printed out a list of eight or nine spots that were not currently booked and would be available until my departure date of March 1, 1999. She assigned another young man with another golf cart who would call back on a walkie-talkie and tell them which spot I had chosen.   Only one spot, on paper, was appealing but we toured them all.   My favorite was on a corner lot.   When we arrived however, a trailer was already parked on it. He called the office and was told "No, it should be empty."

A half-hour of squawking back and forth to each other and computer checking went by before they realized that it was one of the new sites that would be getting a park model, a permanent-type residence.   In plain English, it was not available to me.

We continued to drive around and the more I saw, the less I liked.   I finally decided on one of the sites on the last lettered street, just across from a large, treeless lot that as the season wore on would be filled to capacity (I was told) with transients.   I would be situated between two park models, one fairly modern and well-maintained with a large lanai facing my trailer and the other an old dilapidated rust bucket with an add-on covered porch that should have been swept away during Noah's flood.

It took a half-hour of trying for me to back in around a small palm tree. When that didn't work, I was directed over to the next street to drive my truck and trailer straight across another site, through a ditch and into my spot. Since I had to cross at the highest part of the ditch, I scraped the bottom of my trailer slightly and ended up coming in at an angle.   I didn't care anymore. I was staying put.

Two hours had passed since my arrival.   It was a thousand degrees out with high humidity. I was frustrated to the point of tears.   I was dripping in sweat.   My T-shirt was clinging to me uncomfortably and the elastic waistband on my shorts was digging into my skin leaving raw angry welts around my middle.   I was angrier than a hot and sweaty five year old who had just been told that she had to wait two hours before going in swimming. I wanted nothing more than to go screaming into the office, telling them in no uncertain terms exactly what they could do with that spot, and demand my money back.

It was about that time that another golf cart arrived with two seemingly experienced, older looking men, both dressed in handyman's clothing. Since I had already unhitched my trailer because I was planning on leaving it askew, they asked that I hitch it up again and they would take care of straightening it out.

The tall heavyset one got behind the wheel and pulled the trailer out, running over a corner of the cement patio as he drove. He tried to back it in around that damn palm tree that should have been ripped out long before I got there and which I was now ready to do with my bare hands. He couldn't do it either and secretly I cheered at his ineptness. He drove around to the next street and was going to pull it back through the ditch. They had brought planking with them. With the help of bricks, flat rocks and the wooden boards, placed strategically, they pulled the trailer across the deepest part of the ditch, pulling into the site at the perfect angle. They leveled one side of the trailer with boards. They put the bricks behind and in front of the wheels to keep it from running away from home under its own power. They attached the water and sewer hoses. The tall lean one drove the golf cart back to the office to get an adapter for the electricity. They hooked up the television cable.

Four hours after my arrival I was off to take a shower. It was party time.

Chapter 42

Bitch, Bitch, Bitch

I cleaned up, changed and left the campground early since the place had already pissed me off royally. The party that evening was a potluck so I stopped at the shopping center with my favorite Publix at the corner of Clark Road and Beneva. I knew there was a phone booth within easy walking distance. I had a fist full of quarters, a few dimes just in case the price had gone up and my telephone directory. I called Mary.

"I knew it," she said with a laugh the instant I said hello, "you're here."

"Well, I'm at Publix," I announced, "I'm going to a party."

"When did you arrive?" she asked.

"Got my trailer settled around four," I said.

"You arrived at four, it's five-thirty and you're going to a party," she said, her voice taking on the tone reserved for those few unbelievable circumstances. "Only you could work that fast," she said. "Whose party?"

"Rick Cusolito works at Sun-N-Fun now, he checked me in. The party is a Toastmasters affair," I said.

"Only you," she repeated. "How's the campground?" she asked and immediately got me started on a few of my favorite expletives. That was not the answer she was expecting and we changed the subject quickly so as not to ruin my newly acquired party mood.

I asked about the lecture series that she was setting up on my behalf. I had sent out thirty letters to various service groups, libraries, bookstores, women's groups and the Sarasota Literary Society, all places I had lectured the previous year. I had even sent a letter to the campground I was staying in along with my confirmation and check for the total amount of the spot.

"Three groups wanted a speaker. My heart sank. One of the reasons I had returned with my new book was because I felt it would be easy to set up speaking engagements. Most knew me and liked my easygoing and entertaining style. By the time I got off the phone, I felt rejected, miserable and overwhelming depressed.

I put it out of my mind as best I could. At Publix I picked up a key lime cheesecake, something I had never tasted before. I drove the two blocks from the shopping center and checked my smile in the mirror. Their door was open so I walked into Rick and Susan's small, white bungalow. I got a wonderful reception from so many people I thought I had left behind permanently. There were a lot of new faces around as well and in the typical Toastmasters' tradition, all came over to greet and welcome me. My spirits lifted somewhat during the festivities and I enjoyed being with my old friends.

The semi-formal meeting and party ended around nine-thirty. We were all required to take our contribution home and with so many other desserts, mine was barely touched.

Before leaving the Cusolito household I called Margaret and Doug Drew. With cheesecake minus one slice in hand I went visiting. I was home exhausted just before midnight, the last half-hour of which was spent lost and driving around the sixteen hundred sites of the Hot-and-Humid-N-Not-So-Much Fun campground. By the time I found a couple wandering around at that hour, I was, once again, totally frustrated. They got me back on track with a few simple directions. I found the lake they mentioned, drove the one-lane road that ran along side it, turned off at the last street and finally found my camping spot. A picnic table had been placed under my awning on the patio.

I awoke around four in the morning, my head pounding, my back and every muscle in my body aching. Two Tylenol, one of which contained the PM compound for restlessness, put me back to sleep within minutes. I staggered out of bed in time to shower, dress comfortably and go over to Mary's house. Over bagels and coffee we talked the

171

morning away. She had a couple of errands to run in the afternoon and I tagged along, thoroughly enjoying her company. After picking up my mail and my post office box key at Ned Burke's house (the editor of the magazine I write for, Writer's Guidelines and News) I picked up a fresh batch of mail at the post office. Once back at Mary's home, I made a few phone calls, leaving messages all over town and letting people know my new phone number and that it would be installed in a few days.

That night I met my friends, Joe and Diane Burke, for coffee at Barnes & Noble, another old familiar and comfortable hangout. Joe was especially thrilled with my new book, not only for its appearance and professionalism, but that I had thanked him for his editing advice in the acknowledgment portion of the book.

The next day I spent with Bal Usefoff. After seeing my book, and admiring it in such glowing words, she suggested a book signing at her home. This would be a repeat performance. She did the same when my first book was released and, I must confess I was thrilled. We chose a date in January. I entered the date in my calendar book. That brought the total up to four scheduled lectures and book signings. I would have to get to work as soon as my phone was installed and call all the people I had sent letters to and would have to confirm the ones that had called. What I thought would be an easy job, had turned into another royal pain.

Within a few days in Sarasota, I had called all my friends and had set up meetings and breakfasts or lunches with all of them. Sundays at four were reserved for El Adobe, where the drinking group congregated. I got back into my writing groups at the book stores, at Manatee Community College and my favorite get together with Joe Burke, Al Cooke, Sally Fradkin and Shirley Alger Kaminski. This last one was an informal group that included lunch every Tuesday at the Miami Sub Shop on the Trail in Bradenton. For hours every week we occupied one of their back booths and read our latest efforts.

I went back to work. I called on all the bookstores. I booked lectures at three Books-A-Million stores, Barnes & Noble in Sarasota and Brandon, the Sarasota Literary Society and on the fourteenth of December, briefcase in hand, I marched into the office at Sun-N-Fun and asked for Steve Redman who was responsible for setting up special events at the campground. I was prepared for a lengthy discussion and possible argument. I didn't get one. After giving him my name, I got a handshake, a smile and "let's go into the office and set up a lecture." They had been awaiting my arrival.

Setting up bunches of lectures had not been as difficult nor as frustrating as it had first appeared.

Life at Sun-N-Fun got no better and unfortunately for my friends I verbalized my complaints every chance I got. The people were much too old. Since most had been coming for years and years and years and, just in case I forgot to mention, years, they were very cliquish. Most did not even say "hello" at morning coffee even after looking at me straight in the eye. I continued the morning coffee ritual though because it meant a mile walk each way and I wanted and needed the exercise.

I did enjoy the swimming pool and hot tub however the facilities were located at least half a mile walk from where I was parked so it quickly became a drudge. I could have driven like most but that would have meant driving home in a wet bathing suit which did not appeal to me. I also could have become one of the elite group of campers by renting a golf cart for the length of my stay. Needless to say, I went only when I felt a real urge for a night in the spa.

While setting up the local lectures I started sending out confirmations for all the events I had booked on my way south. Thankfully, I had lots of work keeping me busy. Not only was I working on my lecture series, I was editing my book, already complete in my computer, on my 1994 trip to Turkey. After completing four chapters I made a major decision to put that book on hold in favor of writing this book on my life as a solo RVer. I had heard once too often from fellow campers "No I'm not interested in traveling abroad.

There is too much in this country that I haven't seen yet. No reason to go elsewhere." I felt the book on Turkey wouldn't sell well until I became better known.

At the time of the book signing at Bal's house, I had three completed, not edited, chapters on Kiss This Florida, I'm Outta Here. When Bal asked for a reading from Everyone's Dream Everyone's Nightmare I declined.

"If you want to read the book," I said, "you'll have to buy it. What I would like to read for you, however, is the first chapter of the new book I'm working on and most of you here are in it."

They were thrilled. After reading the chapter I told them the name I had temporarily chosen. Almost everyone laughed. Only my friend Joan Papa commented.

"Aren't you afraid the people in Florida will be upset with that name?" she asked.

"Joan," I answered, "there are people in Florida who love it here. Hopefully, they'll grab the book saying 'what the hell does she mean by that'. There are people here who hate Florida and hopefully they'll grab the book and say 'I know what she means by that'. And Joan," I continued, "there are forty-nine other states that couldn't care less about Florida," I told her.

She seemed appeased.....not pleased.....but appeased.

I spent just short of eleven weeks in Sarasota. I loved seeing and being with my friends. I was delighted to have delivered nineteen lectures to many new people and groups and got wonderful feedback from them. I sold a lot of books. I loved getting back into a few of my writers' groups.

I hated being in Florida. Since I was still considered a local author and supposedly available at all times, I received no radio, television or newspaper coverage despite all my efforts. My only time in front of the television camera was the day of the State of the Union Address at the end of January when I was asked what I thought the president should say that evening. I suggested he say "I quit" commenting on the fact that the United States was one of the most powerful nations in the world and we had a president that can't keep his fly zipped. The newswoman seemed to be taken aback and I was sure my comments would be edited out. When I was stopped over and over again in the campground about my remarks, I knew that I had made it onto the news. I also discovered that it was being shown hourly on SNN, the local all news station. That was my only fifteen minutes of fame for that month.

I hated the campground. On March 1, 1999, around ten o'clock in the morning, my phone already disconnected so I couldn't call to say goodbye, I packed up my camper, rolled out through the gates and didn't look back.....again.

Chapter 43

Party Time

The only good thing out of Florida, the comedian had quipped with a deep raspy voice, is the I-75 heading north. With each mile in that direction I breathed a little easier. I knew exactly what he meant. I felt nothing but relief as I cruised past Bradenton, a few nondescript towns adjacent to the highway and finally Tampa into less familiar territory. The one hundred and eighty-five mile drive took a little over four hours stopping at almost every rest area. As I closed in on Gainesville, I hoped that the campground I had chosen, thirteen miles north of the city, would have easy access off the highway. It did.

I pulled in, paid for five days and drove down a rocky path to my spot. There were only a couple of campers and the place looked rather forlorn. "Don't worry," I was told when I paid for my stay, "it'll be full by about four."

I wasn't worried. I needed some quiet time and my ribs, that I had tried to ignore most of the day, were now throbbing. While cleaning and packing up that morning I had placed the two boards that had been propping up the left side of my camper into the bed of my truck. I had carefully secured one end of the boards with bungy cords and fastened it onto the steel plate housing of the fifth wheel. I tried to do the same at the other end but it required climbing onto a chair and stretching over the side of my truck. I stretched a smidgen too far and felt something pull in the ribcage area at the most inopportune moment. My held my breath as I finished the job.

Four hours later and tense from all the driving that 'something' now ached rather badly and I hoped it would be all right until after I got my trailer unhitched and set up. I stretched out on the bed when the work was all done and unfolded the map of Gainesville. I remembered many of the streets from my first visit and pinpointed the bookstores easily enough. I highlighted them both in yellow. I flipped on the television set and eased into a short nap.....a very short nap. The first time I rolled over, a sharp pain shot through me like I had been poked with a branding iron. I held my breath as I forced myself to a seated position. I took a couple of Tylenol. I walked across the lawn and into the ladies room. I found a clean restroom with large well-equipped shower stalls. I took a long and steaming hot shower that seemed to work its magic and perked me up a bit. Since it was just movement and not breathing that hurt, I paid as little attention as possible to my rib problem. I walked back to my camper and lay down again.

Exhausted from a long, full day, I retired early and fell asleep quickly. Unfortunately I did not sleep well. After a night of tossing and turning and sharp jabs, I was in even more pain the next morning. Out of bed early, I worked slowly and meticulously cleaning up and having breakfast so I would not have to make any extra movements.

I found my daily planner. I made up four flyers for each store where I would be doing a lecture and a little after lunch I drove into Gainesville, fortified with painkillers. I found both stores easily enough. With all my running around, visiting each store personally, talking to each manager and sending out confirmation letters, they had forgotten I was doing a lecture. There would be no problem doing a book signing but nothing had been advertised. Nothing had been done, except for the flyers still in my possession, that each store manager promised they would put up. I was disappointed. In my heart I knew that this was the start of things to come.

I returned to the campground in severe pain, gobbled two more Tylenol, eased my body onto the bed and closed my eyes, the television droning on in the background. I slept while the pills took effect. By the time I was ready to roll off the bed, several campers were parked in the row next to mine and couples were strolling around the grounds. I left my camper. The new arrivals always wandered over to the penned peacocks in the far corner of the lot. There were four in all, plus a few wild birds that flew into the cage for food. One brace was the traditional, multicolored variety. The second was pure white. As if on cue, magnificent tails jutted up and fanned out as they strutted around their pen. We watched in amazement and it usually started an interesting conversation on birds and ended with an even more interesting conversation on where they'd been and what they had seen along the way. The days passed.

It was on the Friday, late in the morning that five motorhomes arrived at the same time. Within an hour three more camping units arrived. By one in the afternoon, several rows were full. When I walked up for my shower, I was motioned over by a couple sitting under their awning.

"What's going on here?" I asked.

"This is a Suwannee Valley Good Sam Rally," the man with a cigarette cupped in his hand said. He put the weed in his other hand when I put my hand out to shake his and told him my name.

"I'm a Good Sammer," I said, "why haven't I been invited?"

"You have now," he replied, "come to dinner tonight."

"I will," I said, breaking into a full grin. "I'd love to join you."

After a light lunch, feeling much better about my lot in life and the day's events, I drove into Alachua. Fortunately the light lunch did nothing to interfere with the samples of thick sliced Keilbasa and smoky, spicy and regular sausage that I gorged on. While I sampled, along with the small group that had assembled to join in the food fest, I talked to the server who had never been more than fifty miles in any direction out of Alachua. She saw no reason to ever leave the area. Even after I had enticed her into listening to a few stories about some of my adventures on the road, she was not impressed. She actually shuttered at the thought of being out there in the world alone.

By the time I left the grocery store, I had restocked my larder and my stomach and had a cheesecake contribution for the potluck dinner with the Good Sam Club. Around five that evening, when I saw the group heading up to the clubhouse, I ventured outdoors. A few looked familiar and Kathy Hubb, the distaff half of the couple I had met that morning introduced me to dark and pretty and easy to talk to Susan Newland. I felt right at home with the warm welcome I had received and was included in all the table conversation after the introductions. Before heading out into a night that was dark as pitch, I was invited back for leftovers the next night. Thankfully several had left the lights on outside their rigs so I was able to maneuver without the benefit of street lamps or moonlight.

The book signings, both of them, were not worth more than a mention that I showed up and did my time. With no advertising and one partially visible flyer (I had hand delivered four of them) that was hidden on a well stocked bulletin board, I expected little. The day was not a total loss. I sold three books at each of the stores and, without a reasonable amount of sales, neither store purchased any extras. One store manager asked if they could keep some of the books on consignment. I declined and volunteered that I was not equipped for that setup and had no way of picking up the books if they didn't sell. I apologized and left the store, more than a little discouraged.

I arrived back at the campground just as the Good Sammers were setting up for leftovers. I was welcomed back by the group. I sold more books that night, under far more enjoyable circumstances, than I did at the bookstores.

Not to be left out of their final get together, I was invited to their 'getaway' breakfast the next morning. I was sorry to see them go. They had been a friendly bunch of hospitable people. I would miss their warmth, the lively conversation and their company. I would also miss being fed.....and fed well. The fact that I didn't have to cook for three days was a big plus in my book. I gave a short thank you speech before breakfast was over and ended with "and who's going to feed me tonight." The laughter was encouraging as was the clapping. Two of the couples printed out their addresses just in case I made it back 'to their neck of the woods.'

Feeling a little lonely, I spent the rest of that Sunday reading and working on my new book. I went for a long walk around the campground and stopped at the only house on the property to see cages full of colorful parrots whose squawking could be heard at the bottom of the hill. I drove into town late that afternoon to fill my tank with fuel.

It was a one hundred and thirty-seven mile drive to Tallahassee the next day. I pulled into the campground and was recognized by the woman behind the desk. She pointed out a great campsite complete with cement patio, that would help keep my camper a little cleaner since the campground was covered in a fine grained sand that turned to mud when it rained.

Return visits seemed to spark a little more appreciation. I liked that.

Chapter 44

The Novices

On my way south, I had received such a pleasant reception from both Barnes & Noble stores and both Books-A-Millions that I had expected a bit of advertising and lots of enthusiasm from the staff. I also looked forward to revisiting Florida's capital, not only for the interesting architecture and quaint downtown area, but for the possibility of being on television again. After checking in with the bookstores I intended calling on the television station that had interviewed me.

Drive days were wasted days for me. No matter what time of the day I arrived in a campground, I always tried to relax on the drive days. Taking down, driving and setting up all on the same day was tough on this old body, especially since everything had to be done manually and with each move I vowed that my next camper would be electric everything whether I could afford it or not.

The day after my arrival I visited all four stores. Even though Books-A-Million had totally forgotten about me, Barnes & Noble actually had me on their monthly Schedule of Special Events calendar to do a Self-Publishing and Promotion lecture.

I awoke early the next day, prepared to start the day with a hearty breakfast so I could skip lunch. My lecture wasn't until one that afternoon. By noon I had one foot out the door, umbrella in hand and open since it was pouring outside. Fortunately my second foot was still in the trailer when I discovered the leak streaming in around my kitchen window, running around the back side of the sink, dribbling off the counter top and pooling on the floor. I put a dry washcloth up against the window frame and watched. Within a few minutes it was saturated.

I removed a giant orange bath towel from the cupboard, gleaned from some hotel in Mexico, folded it over several times and shoved it against the wall to fit snugly behind the sink and propped up by the faucet. Another rolled up towel blocked the trickling on the side of the sink and another one lay folded on the floor. There was nothing more to do and I could wait no longer. I had twenty minutes to get to the store where a huge mob would be waiting to absorb my every pearl of wisdom. There were twenty of my books sitting on a small round table and two chairs had been placed beside it.

As soon as I arrived, I was greeted warmly by the store manager. She promptly informed me that they had forgotten that this was Spring Break and she really did not expect anyone to show up. She was wrong. Other than myself, there were three eager listeners. The lecture I gave was an informal one. Rather then give them the benefit of my vast experience, which they probably didn't want or need, I answered their questions. There was no one seated at the table, except me since I was already working on book number three, that was within striking distance of publishing a book. Their questions concerned finding a publisher, copyright laws, how to get started writing, where to get story ideas and the like. After it was over, I sold one book, autographed the other nineteen, and hurried home to check on the flood. There was none. I would love to admit that my towels had done the trick but that wasn't it. The rain had stopped long before I had arrived at the store.

My fingers ran around the outside perimeter of the offending window. I found a gaping hole where the silicone had pulled away from the trailer. I didn't worry for the moment since the rain had been replaced by sunshine and no more was predicted for the next few days. I made a mental note to get some stuff to repair it.

Within the hour I was out the door heading towards Thomasville. The Books-A-Million had booked a lecture called Solo World Travel. It seems that I was the only one who had remembered the booking. The manager, who had been fascinated by my adventures and promised to do lots of advertising, was off that day. The staff knew nothing about my coming in but they set up a table when I arrived, complete with tablecloth. I brought in my own colorful flyers, perched both books up in two separate piles and proceeded to sit and wait. One of the assistant managers brought me a cup of coffee and a muffin. I sold four books. They purchased three more of each book. I left satisfied with the sales but discouraged with the lack of enthusiasm. I should have been used to it, or at least prepared for it, but I wasn't. It was always a letdown.

That evening was fun in the campground. I met Bill and Kenna. It was their first night in a brand new Starflyte, a self-contained motorhome that I had looked at myself. When we met they were walking around the outside of their pride and joy looking at all the connections and making sure everything was hooked up properly. I thought they were having some kind of a problem so when I stopped to chat I asked if they needed help, from me.....the expert.

I was invited in for a glass of wine. I accepted. Their old golden retriever rested at my feet and I bent down to scratch an ear every time he looked up at me. With a dog in residence it was difficult to smell the newness, but it was sparkling clean. Although they had a made-up bed at the back, they had no table so meals would have to be served on trays or a lap, which they didn't seem to mind.

"We don't plan on cooking much," Bill volunteered.

It was around eight-thirty when they left to go out to dinner and I returned to my camper. It was pitch dark so my evening stroll was over. With the help of the wine and a day of running around, I fell asleep within the hour.

It was early the next morning when I peeked out my window to see what the hubbub was about. Bill and Kenna were unhooking for the first time. Bill, wearing spanking new rubber gloves especially for the occasion, held the plug high in the air while he gave a running commentary on each step of the operation. Kenna was filming each move and gesture and if she didn't like a particular angle she made Bill repeat it. The performance went on for close to an hour. A group, all used to the daily process of campground life, had gathered round and everyone enjoyed the antics of the novices.

I spent the rest of the day doing chores. I cleaned my camper. I did several loads of laundry. I drove to the Flying J, three exits west and twelve miles away, to fill up with diesel and at three that afternoon I went to my last book signing at Books-A-Million. I stayed until seven and sold four books. The assistant manager suggested that if I wasn't busy, I should return the next day around eleven in the morning because the lunch hour was usually very busy. The next morning I sold six books and just as I was cleaning up around three in the afternoon, the manager came in and suggested that since Thursday night was really, really busy, I might want to come back. I returned that night around eight stayed until closing and did no business whatsoever. I was not unhappy to be on my way.

It was an easy drive to Dothan, Alabama. I stopped at one rest area only. I met a middle-aged couple, Ed and Cookie, who were in the process of moving from California to Florida. Since they wondered why I was traveling alone I told them my story. They bought a copy of each of my books and promised to write.

I pulled into the campground in Dothan. I paid for two nights of camping. After unhitching, I got back into my truck and drove to Wal-Mart to pick up a tube of silicone, a few groceries and a new watchband. I had been gone a couple of hours. When I returned the place was swarming with police cars.

Chapter 45

To Cheat A Stranger

"What's going on?" I asked the two anorexic-looking blonds standing outside a small, unkempt trailer, each hand holding onto either the tiny hand of a child or a cigarette.

"A black man stole a purse in the supermarket and he's hidin' in them woods," one of them answered showing darkened wide-spaced teeth. "He's wearin' a white shirt, that's all we know," she continued.

I stood watching for a minute or two then returned to the truck to remove the groceries and get them under refrigeration. I took out my lounge chair and placed it close to the road so I could see what was going on in comfort. We were all glued for over an hour but nothing happened. One policeman came out of the woods with a German Shepherd on a leash and one by one the half dozen police cars pulled out. They didn't return that day or the next. If they caught the guy, we never heard. Nothing was mentioned on the news that evening.

Late that afternoon I drove to the Books-A-Million store. According to my calendar my autographing session was scheduled from four to six the next day. With all my recent experience I knew the bookstore had done nothing in preparation. I asked if I could come in earlier. The next day was a Saturday and people would be in and out all day, I thought. They didn't mind at all if I took advantage of the situation.....as a matter of fact, they seemed enthused.

It was still light when I arrived home and a beat up rented motorhome was parked beside mine sporting information on the back as to where to rent this 'beauty'. The driver was a dark-haired, slim man in his forties. His wife, slim but heavier boned and equally as dark, was checking around on the ground outside their motorhome. Something was leaking, I could see. It turned out to be water from their hot water tank.

"Can I help?" I asked.

"No von can help," he answered giving me a smile. "I must turn off the vater," he said with a German accent. "Dis motorhome is no good. Missing much pieces and too big to drive in city." he said.

"Where did you get it?" I asked.

"Ve ordered it through a company in Germany. Ve asked for a little camper and they guarantee us von. Vhen ve arrived, dis is all they had. Take it or leave it," they said. He continued talking as we walked around the perimeter.

The camper, a thirty-eight foot Bounder, had dents and scratches and missing lights. The screens were broken and stuffed into a storage compartment in one of the outside bins. Two or three of the windows were cracked. The water hose was broken and leaked like a sieve not only where it was attached to the camper. Mini fountains spouted from several spots on the hose as it snaked along the ground to the outside connection. The ground was becoming muddy from the spillage. What I loved best about it, however, was that it had a temporary license plate taped onto the back window that had expired over a year before.

"You can't drive it this way," I advised them. We walked up to the road and used the pay phone to call the 800 number that was listed on the camper. No one answered. "We'll call again tomorrow," I assured them, "and I'll talk to them for you."

The next day was a busy one for both of us. My German friends were visiting Dothan because their nineteen year old daughter was an exchange student and they were meeting the host family for breakfast. I left the campground around noon and returned a little after six in the evening. My neighbors did not return that evening although their motorhome was still parked there. Obviously their hosts had picked them up. I saw no reason to call the 800 number again since I didn't have the paperwork or even the location where they had rented it. For that matter I didn't even know their names. The evening before was the last time I saw of them.

The rain started around nine that night, slowly at first. It didn't take long to intensify into a major storm. My trailer was suddenly shaking from the relentless wind that gusted up to fifty miles per hour at times and the pelting down of the huge drops sounded more like hail when it hit the roof. I worried that the heavy gauge plastic vents would not hold back the onslaught. I stayed glued to the television set. Tornadoes were making earthly contact all around the area. Although none touched anywhere close to the campground, I didn't sleep much.

It was hard to believe that after the dreadful thunderstorms of the night before that it would be sunny and bright in the morning. The sunshine and the fact that I had done well at the bookstore the day before served to lift my spirits. I cleaned up, packed up and was on the road early. I wasn't going far that day and since I was traveling on a Sunday, when traffic would be lessened, I decided to look for the campground gleaned from my Woodall's directory, a guide I rarely used. This campground was located less than fifteen miles north of Montgomery. My familiar spot in Troy would have meant a forty mile drive each way. I decided to test out new territory.

Despite the sunny start to the day the black clouds producing rain showers plagued me most of my journey. I arrived mid-afternoon and although the campground did not have the charm or cleanliness of Troy I decided to book in for three days. I was getting tired from the constantly pulling up stakes and decided on a short break since I had the time. I would clean up and shower in my camper and not use the campground facilities anyway. Despite the lack of clean washrooms, the campground was crowded and usually filled to capacity by nightfall.

My book signing was on a Monday. I had been told that Mondays were exceptionally busy. I arrived around three-thirty, set up close to the front door around four and was promptly forgotten about by the staff. I stayed until ten and did surprising well. The manager came over late in the evening, apologized for not paying more attention and we talked for a long time.

"Most authors" he said, "are such a pain in the ass. They want everything delivered immediately and demand to be served coffee on a regular basis. They want the table manned by our staff when they have to leave for a minute. You're so quiet," he said, "we forgot about you."

I couldn't help but thank him. They had said the same in all the other stores I had been in and all the Books-A-Million stores, including this one, had invited me back anytime I was in the area. They would make a special effort to accommodate me whenever I was in town. Not only had I done well, the manager of the store purchased seven more books to make the final count twenty books. I filled out the invoice and they paid me in cash directly from the register. By the time I left the store it was pitch dark and I was glad that I only had a twelve mile highway drive back to the campground.

I rewarded myself with one complete day off. I drove over the highway into Prattville. I browsed Office Depot, Bookland and a Super Wal-Mart. I relaxed over lunch, enjoying the best crispy-crunchy fried chicken with biscuits I had ever tasted. I bought a new two-cup coffee maker, since my old one, and I mean really old one, had started hitting and missing as far as the electricity was concerned. I returned home a few minutes before my neighbor, Frankie Morrison of Laurel, Montana knocked on my door and asked if I would like to walk up the road to four or five antique shops. It was such a pleasant way to spend my day off.

By the next morning I was ready to hit the road.

Chapter 46

A Day of Sadness

It was an easy drive on that St. Patrick's Day Wednesday. The weather was warm and bright and not a hint of a cloud in the sky. It was a mere hundred or so miles that I had to drive back to Gardendale, twelve miles north of Birmingham. The only major pain was the highway driving directly over the heart of the city. The ridges across the road, caused by I can only assume years of repair work, for about twenty or more miles bounced the truck and trailer. Since the wheels of each hit at different intervals it produced a rocking effect that jangled my nerves and finally bobbed my head to the point of headache. I was thrilled when I finally reached the north side of the city where the highway improved tremendously.

It was a relief the pull into the familiar campground. I checked in at the office but it was closed. A caretaker, one that I had not met on my previous trip, suggested I pull into any vacant spot. After looking them all over I found my spot. I was out leveling the trailer when I discovered that I was facing the wrong direction and all the services were on the opposite side of the trailer. I pulled out and drove around the campground but couldn't seem to turn sharply enough to get back into the spot. I finally pulled out onto the street and into the parking lot of the funeral parlor across the road. I did a giant u-turn in their lot, drove back out onto the street and into the campground. I returned to my chosen spot and this time everything was within easy attaching distance. I unhitched.

It was hours later when Martha returned. Louise's husband had died the day before, she told me. Although they were long divorced, they had remained good friends and his unexpected death, after a very short illness, had devastated the family. Louise arrived a few minutes after Martha. We all went out for a late lunch. It was a quiet one and mostly I just listened. Although I was invited along to take care of incidentals concerning the funeral arrangements, I declined and spent the rest of the day in or around my camper.

When I went into the office the next morning Barney was there alone. Not much was going on and little was expected. While the family went to the funeral, I stayed in the office and manned the phones. Only Barney called once to see if all was well. I advised him that two campers had checked in and I had handled it. By the time he returned it was early afternoon. I had completed one chapter of my new book, played several computer games and was ready for lunch. Barney had returned with chicken nuggets from a local fast food eatery and we shared them.

The afternoon was devoted to personal shopping. I had my hair cut short, something that always gave me a lift. I deposited the receipts from my book sales into the bank, a branch of which was close to the beauty salon. It took a little running around but I finally found an item I had been looking for.....a hot air popcorn machine.

That weekend was especially busy. I accomplished four book signings in three days. On that Saturday I raced from the Wildwood store directly to the Brook Highland store. All four of the stores put my table, complete with tablecloth, close to the front doors and let me greet their customers. I brought twenty copies of each book into every store with me (of course the back seat of my truck groaned under the weight of hundreds more should I be so lucky as to sell out and need to acquire more at a moment's notice). I also printed up my own flyers to make a colorful addition to the table.

Only after I left the Brook Highland store did I run into a bit of trouble. I was so sure I could find my way back to Interstate 65 without going back the way I had come since it seemed to be a long way around. I was wrong. The map was wrong. After one turn off a major road, I ran out of four lane roads and ended up on small side streets long after dark. I kept coming back to streets with stores on them but when the stores started looking familiar I realized I was going in circles. I didn't know how to find my way back to the main street. At a traffic light I rolled down my window and asked the lady sitting in the passenger seat in the car that had pulled up beside me for directions back to the Interstate. After some conversation between she and her companion, they suggested I follow them. They were going right by it, she told me. I followed and it didn't take long for me to become unnerved. They were driving through a housing development. The streets were narrow, lined with parked cars and they turned onto side streets even smaller than the ones we had just left. Several of the roads curved around a park. I was really becoming nervous and debated if I should continue following. It was just about that time that we turned onto a major city road and I actually recognized it as the one I had traveled from Wildwood to Brook Highland. I beeped and waved as I pulled off that main road and onto the Interstate. They will never know how grateful I was.

It was on the Monday morning that I said goodbye to Barney and Martha and asked them to convey my condolences to Louise who never did come back to the campground. It was an uneventful four-hour drive back to Nashville. I was delighted when I pulled into my favorite Two Rivers Campground on Music Valley Drive. I got instant recognition and a warm greeting from tall, dark and very handsome Troy Perry, who handed me a large package of mail, with "it just arrived this morning" said in his best western twang.

It didn't take long to unhitch, go for groceries and make a bunch of phone calls. It was the start of two weeks of nonstop work.

Chapter 47

Getting My Fill

I loved being back in Nashville. It didn't take me long to get in touch with Red. I also called Wanda from my favorite Toastmasters' Club. She and I arranged to meet one day for lunch so she gave me directions to get to her office. That was the last free moment I had.

I drove to Premium Press America and was greeted by Bette with "your ears must have been burning" as she handed me a check for the sale of the first fifty books through the distributor. "Although Everyone's Dream has not yet been accepted by any head office," George explained, "it is still under review." I was a little discouraged. It was beginning to sink in that the road to self-publishing was filled with hills and valleys and with each hill climbed more dirt was shoveled on top.

I needed some good news. I drove out to Home Depot in Madison to see Red and Ray. Both were manning the phones and we talked in between calls. Ray informed me that a new Jayco Dealership was opening just down the road and Red suggested that I talk to the owners about setting up a book signing. "Since both your books are on travel, they will fit in nicely," he said. I didn't need much convincing especially after being told how congenial they were.

Before going to the Jayco Dealership, I stopped into the Books-A-Million to find out that they were expecting me in April but nothing was advertised concerning a lecture, it would be strictly a signing. What the hell, I was learning to roll with the punches.

At Camper's Corner, a weekend away from their Grand Opening, I was given the typical Nashville greeting by owner Raymond Brody and his sister Paige. When I explained that Red and Ray from Home Depot had suggested I contact him, he was thrilled to hear that they were both coming to the opening. They would be delighted to set up a

192

table for me and I could sell to my hearts content. And "no, they would not accept a commission on the sale of my books. Whatever I sold would be mine. It would be their pleasure to have me as their guest."

What could I say except "thank you, I'll be there."

By the time I got back to my camper it was early evening and raining. I stayed inside the rest of the night.

On the way to Wanda's office I stopped at Bookstar. Up on the theater marquee it said World Travel Seminar on Wednesday, March 31, 7:00 P.M. According to my records, Bookstar was where I was doing a Self-publishing and Promotion lecture while at Barnes & Noble in Brentwood I would be doing a Solo World Travel lecture. I went into the store and picked up a bulletin to discover my first and last name spelled incorrectly, i.e. Joci Hassock and my middle name omitted completely. I was suddenly relieved that my name had not been put up on the marquee for all the world to see since my own mother would not have recognized it.

A Chinese buffet lunch with Wanda consisted of mediocre food and lots of fun talk of family, friends, Toastmasters along with business ideas and travel plans. Visiting with a friend soothed my wounded ego and lifted my spirits. On the way back to the campground I stopped into Davis-Kidd hoping to see my book on their shelf. No such luck. It was late afternoon when I got home. I was tired, a bit annoyed, slightly discouraged and ravenous. Wandering the campground after a light vegetarian dinner I met Joyce and Wayne from Illinois. It was a pleasant way to pass the hours, exchanging camping stories and, for the moment, forgetting about the writing/publishing/lecturing business.

I spent two days working the dealership opening. The party, complete with trays upon trays of a variety of cold cuts, cheeses, pickles, olives and relishes and bite sized vegetables with dips, an assortment of breads, buns and crackers was a major success for the Brody's. No sooner was one tray emptied it was replaced by a freshly stocked one. Karaoke music played in the background with customers trying their best. One or two of the participants, including Paige, had wonderful singing voices. When asked if I would like to be included in the sing along, I suggested I take the microphone just before closing. That would guarantee a quick finish to the festivities with customers climbing over each other to get out of the building and into the melodious Nashville street traffic. They all laughed.

It was a terrific party but few sales. I left early on Saturday and went over to Books-A-Million. I asked if I could set up a book signing for Sunday from four to six o'clock since they had another author coming in from two to four. I arrived at three the following afternoon in the hopes of sneaking a peek at my predecessor. I met Frances Jordan Beard, author of Nothing to Lose and Kith and Kin, also from Sarasota. We not only chatted like old friends but we exchanged bits and pieces of information on our lives as authors, publishers and promoters. We both agreed that publishing a second book brought renewed interest in the first book. She used the same catchy phrase that I did....."No one can buy just one," going along with the potato chip commercial.

When six o'clock rolled around, and traffic seemed to increase, I asked if I could stay longer since going home would mean sitting around my empty trailer. The manager didn't seem to mind and by the end of the evening I had sold eight books. Also I had met some interesting people to talk to, including a rather attractive, single man I had spoken to the day before at the Jayco dealership. I was certainly getting around. I was definitely learning a few things like the fact that there was another Books-A-Million in Murfreesboro, about forty miles south east of Nashville.

Late morning, the following day, I drove out to Murfreesboro. The bookstore was easy to find thanks to directions supplied the evening before but the manager would not be in until after one. I had a couple of hours to kill. I walked to Wendy's at the far end of the shopping center. The two ladies behind me in line at the restaurant were the same two ladies behind me in line at Books-A-Million. After a little small talk, I asked if I could sit with them and have my lunch. They were delighted. The conversation, after exchanging snippets of our lives, became something out of a mystery novel. An old cousin of theirs, living in Pensacola, Florida had gone out for a short ride in his old truck on January twenty-sixth of that year. His truck was found four miles into the bush. He had vanished without a trace. Unlike a mystery novel however, not everything in life has to make sense or have an ending. This story didn't. The old man was never found.

That was the last story we exchanged. We said our good byes and parted.

Angie Henderson, the manager, was a dark-haired, enthusiastic, fireball with one deep dimple in her cheek. We got along from the instant we met. She immediately purchased five of each of my books that she set up on a table along side a stack of book marks and it had been arranged for me to come in that Thursday.

The lecture at Barnes & Noble in Brentwood didn't happen. The store was in the midst of renovations and there was no place to put rows of chairs. They put a stack of my book, Everyone's Dream, on a table and parked me near the entrance. A few people came to chat. One couple, headed overseas for an extended vacation like the one I had taken, wanted a lecture. I gave them an abbreviated version and answered all their questions. I sold a few books and autographed the rest.

The lecture at Bookstar the next night bordered on bizarre. The table and chairs were all neatly placed and a couple of people were waiting. One was a young, pretty girl dressed in office garb. She had come directly from work and was leaving for England the following week. The man sitting several seats away was old and paunchy. What little hair he had was gray and wispy. Everyone wanted to talk. No one wanted to listen. I asked and answered questions for the young woman. The old man, a retired priest, was hell bent on telling us of his travels to Morocco, most of Europe and parts of Asia. In the end he bought two books which I autographed for him. Within minutes the store clerk came back to the young girl and handed her one of my books that the priest had paid for. Bizarre. After the lecture a few more customers came by to chat. Each conversation started with "they were sorry they had missed my lecture." They too purchased books. I autographed the rest. The entire evening was a strange one.

The book signing at Murfreesboro did not go well. "This is a slow night," Angie explained. "Why not come back tomorrow," she said, "I'm on duty." I told her I had numerous errands to run in the morning and would be back mid afternoon. She was delighted.

I stopped into Premium Press for a long talk with George. I went to Vaughan Printing to see if they remembered me and was greeted with a hug from David Prentice. When Jean returned we all reminisced for over an hour. Jean was in the middle of reading my book. I got a glowing, almost page by page, report of what she liked and she insisted that I answer her numerous questions. She loves travel stories and I loved being quizzed about it.

I drove back to Murfreesboro. I did a little better and Angie was so impressed with my story she decided to feature Everyone's Dream in the Sales Pick Area of the store. In addition to the books sold she purchased ten more copies. She also booked a lecture on Self-Publishing and Promotion for the end of November when I would be once again heading south. I returned home, shall we say, a happy camper.

The next day, Saturday, I did a book signing at Books-A-Million in Madison. The constant work and not much fun was catching up to me. I was tired and cranky. I needed a day off and when that same store asked if I wanted to return the next day, I declined. I desperately needed to rest and regroup.

I took that Sunday off, if you can call it that. In the evenings, when I wasn't too tired or it wasn't too late, I would wander the campground. I sold almost as many books in the campground as I did at the bookstores. That Sunday was the same. I ended up having a mini wine and cheese party with newlywed couple Jack and Carol Messick, both in their late fifties. She had been widowed from a very happy marriage and had been single many years. "My children were starting to worry about me," she said. "I had lost a lot of weight," she confessed, "and was becoming reclusive. Once I met Jack," she said, "my life changed. I think I have gained about twenty pounds," she said looking at him and smiling.

"Yes," he replied, "I think I'm about twenty pounds happier too."

They were easy to talk to, laughed heartily at my jokes, told several of their own and the entire evening just slipped by nibbling on various cheeses, crackers, pickles and large, salted pretzels and washed down with my contribution to the party, a large bottle of Burgundy.

Meeting them was just the treat I needed to end my stay in Nashville.

Chapter 48

I'd Walk A Mile For An Ice Cream

Although I was not going far, I was up early packing, cleaning and trying to get someone from the office to fill my propane tanks. It was a chore and I was relieved when it was finally done since I had been trying for a couple of days to get someone to fulfill a simple request. On the Saturday the young man had waited too long and then simply forgot about me. On Sunday the propane station, operated by the Cullum and Maxey RV's, our next door neighbor and owner of the campground where I was staying, did not open at all. Monday was my last chance and I really needed them filled before getting on the road.

I attached the trailer, rode around the park and didn't like the way the brakes sounded or felt. When they weren't grabbing, send me careening towards the windshield, they felt spongy. I played with the braking unit located within easy reach under my ashtray and was not really satisfied with the results. I got on the road anyway.

There wasn't much traffic. I had driven about thirty miles when I pulled into the first rest area. I fiddled with the trailer brakes again and they suddenly seemed to adjust properly. I can't be sure but perhaps they needed the drive to warm up. The rest of the trip was comfortable and uneventful. Since this was my second visit to the Elizabethtown KOA, I knew exactly where it was, pulled in, paid, drove down to the bottom of the hill and settled myself. I was back in the same spot as the year before.

I had been there only about fifteen minutes when a trailer pulled in along side sporting Ohio plates. Pat held onto the leash of an old greyhound while Clark set up their trailer. They were obviously experience and it didn't take them long. Since I had entered a new time zone when I hit Elizabethtown, Kentucky, I knew it would stay light a wee bit longer.

Being the second visit, I also knew that the mini market and gas station within an easy walk had the best ice cream I had tasted in a long while. I also had a bunch of letters to mail so I asked if they wanted to go for a walk. Pat was delighted. Clark declined. Within minutes we were on our way. The mail box was right in front of the station and the Pralines and Cream ice cream was exactly as I had remembered.....creamy, crunchy and delicious and a little over a dollar's worth was enough to ruin dinner. "Eat your dessert first," I have always been told, "just in case you don't live through the meal." It is a motto I now live and breathe by.

By the time we returned, dinner had to be prepared, the sun was slowly going down and black clouds had parked themselves directly overhead and were not moving. We said good night and wished each other well since we probably would not be seeing each other in the morning. They planned on leaving before the sun was up since they were one day away from home and anxious to get back. The rain started after dark, was not loud or lingering, and was over before the sun came up the next morning. In the dark I heard my neighbors pull out.

I had never unhitched so it was going to be an easy getaway. I disconnected the water and electricity, rolled my trailer up to the dump station, finishing the job of cleaning up. I left my trailer parked there while I went to wash my hands before getting onto the highway. Again I was not going far.

The morning was perfect. The sun was shining. It was bright and clear and not a cloud in the sky. There was almost no traffic on the road.

Chapter 49

The End Of The Road

What the hell was that! My mind snapped into high gear, as did my truck. I struggled to maintain control as everything bucked and jolted forward. I looked out at both side mirrors and saw nothing in either one of them. In that same split second I thought the tires had gone flat on the trailer and I was dragging it along the highway. I could not imagine what was happening. I looked down at the odometer to see 18.8 miles. I rolled off onto the shoulder. I looked back down the highway as I got out of the truck. I saw nothing. I walked towards the rear.

It was a gold Marquis with Michigan plates that pulled off directly behind me. The couple appeared to be in their mid-forties. They both got out of the car and I could see that his air bag had deployed. She did not say a word, stunned into silence.

"I have no idea what happened," he said over and over. "Are you okay?" he asked. "Are your passengers okay?" he asked without waiting for an answer. "Let's go check on your passengers," he said.

"I'm alone and yes, I'm okay," I answered almost in a whisper.

"I don't know what happened," he said again. "I didn't see you."

"How could you not see me?" I asked, not really expecting an answer. "I'm pulling a house behind that truck and I'm the only thing on the road. How could you not see me?"

I walked to my truck, extracted my newly acquired cell phone and dialed 911. When the operator answered, I asked if they could send out a patrol car and "thank you, no, we don't need an ambulance, no one's hurt."

"I don't know how this happened," he said again.

His dark-haired, pretty wife looked ashen standing silently beside the car.

I surveyed the damaged. His car had smashed dead center into the back of my trailer, crushing the flimsy bumper and caving in the aluminum rear panels. The spare tire remained intact, but now hung at an odd angle as the top of the tire extended past the bumper. I walked to the side and took down the two steps so I could assess the damage inside and, before entering, noticed that where the bed part of the trailer jutted out over the truck, there was a new wrinkle in the aluminum. I opened the door. At the new outside wrinkle, part of the wall panel had separated from the siding inside. I climbed over the boxes that I always placed on the floor so they wouldn't fall, opened the door to the bathroom and discovered the wooden cabinet, that surrounded the sink, had been smashed to smithereens. Not much else looked out of place. I went back outside to wait for the police.

As soon as my hand went up to my head, he asked again. "Are you sure you don't want to sit down, you really don't look well."

"I have a headache," I responded, grateful for his concern, "I'll be okay."

The patrol car arrived within minutes. The driver of the gold Marquis again repeated to the policeman, "I don't know how this happened. I didn't see it."

"What didn't you see, sir?" asked the officer, giving the three of us standing there the once over.

"That," he said, pointing to the camper.

"What do you mean you didn't see it. Who was driving?" asked the officer.

"I'm driving the car," he answered.

"The trailer is mine," I volunteered.

"Are you driving that thing alone?" he asked, suddenly becoming far more concerned.

"Yes," I responded.

"Let's go check the inside," he said.

"There doesn't seem to be much damage inside," I said as we both wandered over, checking the rear before going inside.

The police reports took about half an hour with each of us showing drivers' licenses, registrations and insurance. We all exchanged telephone numbers and addresses and I had the officer give me his card complete with name, badge number and pertinent telephone numbers. The number of the report was also written on the card. There was nothing left to do at the scene. I got back into the truck, started it and took off, my mind in a whirl and a headache starting to grab hold.

I drove to Walton, Kentucky trying to keep my mind focused on the drive and not on the accident that was starting to unravel me. It was exactly one hundred and thirty-seven miles to the campground and I was acutely aware of each mile. I was relieved when I turned onto the road leading up to the office. I paid for a couple of nights of camping. I asked if Larry, the man who had helped me back it in the last time, could back the trailer onto a spot because I had just been hit and didn't feel like handling the aggravation. Within minutes the trailer was parked. I unhitched.

I took a couple of Tylenol, gathered up my insurance information and headed for the telephone around the corner from the office. I dragged a chair out from under a patio table and made myself as comfortable as I could. I called my insurance company. When they suggested that an insurance adjuster would be out within a week or so, I asked if the adjuster could come to a campground in Erie, Pennsylvania. "That will be where I'm doing my last lecture," I said.

"Sure, we can send him anywhere in the United States but please take the trailer in someplace and make sure that it's towable," said Doug White.

"Why shouldn't it be towable," I said with an indignant flare, "I towed it to here, didn't I."

"Humor me," came the reply, "find a garage and have them take a look at it."

"Okay," I said, "there's one just up the street about a mile away."

Tuesday was a lost day. My head pounded and I gobbled painkillers at regular intervals. I was nervous about getting back into the camper and felt one day off to catch my breath and rid myself of the headache wouldn't hurt. I went out to lunch at the Flying J gas station about a mile north of the campground. Right across from Flying J was a RV dealership, Delightful Days. I went into the service department and explained about the accident.

"Could you just look it over and make sure it's towable before I get back on the highway. You don't have to do anything, just let me know if I can take it on the highway safely. I'm driving to Erie, Pennsylvania," I said.

"Sure can," said the young, burly guy in oil stained overalls.

"I'll bring it in just after you open," I said.

At eight-thirty the next morning I was waiting at the door when they opened. My trailer remained road ready in their parking lot. Two young mechanics lay flat on their backs under the camper speaking in muffled tones. I couldn't make out what was being said. They came out from under together.

"Lady," said the one I had spoken to the day before, "how the hell did you get this thing here. The trailer will make it to Erie. The wheels won't."

Except for the one mile drive back to the campground, it was the end of the road.

203

Epilogue

It was indeed the end of the road.....but only for the twenty-two and a half foot fifth wheel Wanderer. For the gutsy broad behind the wheel of the F-250 Ford diesel it was only the beginning.

The insurance adjuster arrived at the campground the following Monday. In looking at the rear of the trailer he said "No problem, they'll just replace these two panels," he said, pointing to the back of the trailer, "and repair the bumper."

"Look closer," I suggested.

I had taken the week of waiting to go over the trailer from the flimsy back end to the sturdy hitch and had found all the subtle changes in the frame. The rear, of course, had sustained the obvious major damage. Where the fifth wheel jutted out, that held the bed above the truck, had been crunched on the outside and that was where the inside wall had pulled away from the aluminum. The steel bar that held the fifth wheel arm onto the trailer frame was bent. The floor supporting my bed had dropped away from the front of the trailer exposing the full length of the nails and the wood underneath. The front steel bar that held the fifth wheel hitch into the bed of the truck was lifted up about half an inch.

The adjuster did take a closer look. On his back he inspected the underneath. I could hear him speaking into his pocket recorder listing all the damage and wondered silently what the outcome of his report would be. "This is gone," he said, the minute he came out from under, after a closing statement or two into the recorder. "The entire frame is bent, not worth repairing."

After the adjuster left, I packaged up the blow-up male doll my friends Mary Mau and Margaret Drew had given me at my going away party. The note that accompanied my non verbal, non responsive, non anything companion read:

"Please, Mary, can I come live with you.

I come from a broken home.

All I need is the occasional blow (up) job.

The quarter in my back pocket is for you for being a good girl.

Please, please, please Mary can I come live with you."

I went to the post office and mailed it. By mid afternoon my bag was packed. The trailer was cleaned. The refrigerator was emptied except for what I needed for dinner. I watched television that evening for the last time in my trailer. I also arranged with the owners for a month of storage somewhere in the park where it would all be safe and secure. Except for one bag of clothes and toiletries and my computer and printer, everything else I owned would remain intact until I could return.

The following morning I was up and ready early. I pulled the trailer to the bottom of the hill where it would be stored. I asked Larry to drive it up the hill and then back it into the spot. I was shocked when he drove it away. The wheels were at such an odd angle that angels must have been riding on my shoulder when I pulled it that one hundred and thirty-seven miles. There was absolutely no reason in the world why that trailer did not collapse in on itself.

I said goodbye to the owners and to Larry, thanking them for all their help. I drove to Erie, Pennsylvania and received a warm welcome from Norene Nungsten. I checked into the motel that Norene recommended after telling her about my adventures. I soaked in a hot tub for an hour or so and enjoyed every luxurious moment. That night I called my friend Arlene Kravitz in Toronto. "I have some good news and I have some bad news," I said to her.

"Oh hell, better give me the good news first," she responded.

"Well," I quipped, "my friends no longer call me trailer trash."

"Why?" she asked.

"Because I'm homeless," I responded giving her some of the details of the accident.

"You always have a home here," she said.

"I know," I answered and I already have the keys to your apartment. "Thank you."

I awoke the next morning, having spent the first night in a bed not my own, feeling mildly like I had slept wrong. It was now about a week and a half after the accident. I went rapidly down hill from there.

The lecture and book signing went well. It had also been arranged that I do a live radio interview, my first one. I was feeling very much the celebrity since colorful flyers had been placed in almost every store window in town.

By the time I arrived in Toronto, the next day, I was living on painkillers. My head, neck and shoulders were stiff and sore. I was afraid to move for fear of the jarring pain that followed. A couple of doctor's appointments, a few X-rays, lots of ice packs and a week of physiotherapy and hourly home exercise improved my situation immensely.

In the two weeks of being in an apartment, I discovered something fascinating.....I didn't like home living one little bit. When I wasn't at physiotherapy or working on my book or visiting friends, I was bored. When I finished my computer work for the day there was no opening the door and finding friends or fellow campers who were in a spot for a day or two and who had interesting stories of their own to tell. I was alone with my pain, my thoughts and a television set. Arlene worked long hours and wasn't home much.

That second week I started making phone calls. I was looking for a truck camper. I didn't want to pull anything anymore. I wanted one piece and I wanted to keep my truck. I had picked up a camping magazine that had made an in depth study of the newest truck campers and from what I saw in the pictures, I needed nothing more.

On the third of May, having driven down to Michigan for that purpose, I purchased a 1999 Elkhorn, ten foot truck camper by Fleetwood. On the sixth it had been fitted onto the back of my truck and I had driven, that same day, the three hundred miles back to Walton, Kentucky.

I arrived early evening and removed from my old trailer the bedding, my coffee maker, a cup, coffee, sugar and other bits and pieces that I would need first thing the next morning. Seven grueling hours of packing, moving and unpacking over a four-day period and twenty-two and a half feet of belongings jam packed into sixteen feet of truck camper space. The six additional feet of space was my bed that sat precariously over the cab of my truck. On the morning of the last load I drove back to Ypsilanti, Michigan and unloaded some of the belongings that hadn't been touched in a year into my storage unit. The camper went back to the dealer to be fitted for an air conditioner and a generator that I had already paid for.

Three days later I drove back to Niagara Falls, Ontario to recuperate. I was exhausted. The entire ordeal had taken six weeks.

I love my new home. Although it is quite a bit smaller, there seems to be more usable and practical space. It is much easier to drive and I am far less intimidated on the road. With a window at the front and back of the camper, I can see right through from the driver's seat to traffic directly behind me. If someone gets too close, I'll jump into another lane. No more sneaking up on me, thank you very much.

I attended my first Escapee RV Club camping rally in Peterborough, Ontario in early June. I am at my second camping rally in Iron Mountain, Michigan having stopped en route for three days to see Marie and Dean Stratton in Gaylord, Michigan. When I told Dean of my travels since we were parked across from each other on that first horrible day in my life as a solo full-timer, he said, "Man do you get around. The biggest town I've been in since the last time I saw you is Wal-Mart."

I'll be attending two rallies in Escanaba, Michigan in a few days before meeting some friends in Hurley, Wisconsin. From there I'm heading to Madison, Wisconsin to visit with friends and to enjoy my first International Good Sam Rally.

When the Grim Reaper comes, I want him to have to look for me. I'm not going to be sitting around waiting for him.

See you all down the road apiece.

By The Same Author

RESTLESS FROM THE START
(A Collection of Short Stories)

ISBN Number: 0-9657509-0-6

Library of Congress Number: 97-91654

U.S. Funds: $10.95 plus $3.50 Postage and Handling
Florida residents add 7% Sales Tax

EVERYONE'S DREAM EVERYONE'S NIGHTMARE

ISBN Number: 0-9657509-1-4

Library of Congress Number: 98-90573

U.S. Funds: $13.95 plus $3.50 Postage and Handing
Florida residents add 7% Sales Tax

Available from: Skeena Press
                       P.O. Box 19071,
                       Sarasota, Florida 34276-2071
                       E-Mail: SkeenaPress@Hotmail.com

                       Also available through Amazon.Com

ABOUT THE AUTHOR:

Joei Carlton Hossack was born and raised in Montreal, Quebec, Canada. She has lived in Toronto, Los Angeles and Sarasota, Florida. She has spent much of the last eleven years traveling the world. She is currently a solo, full-time RVer, writing, lecturing and entertaining as she travels both Canada and the United States.

She is a columnist for RVGroupwise, The Vagabond Chronicles and The Gypsy Journal.

Check out her web site:

www.concentric.net/~Lmchaney/author/Joei.htm

She can be reached at: JoeiCarlton@Hotmail.com